LifeLaunch
Student's Handbook

Jan Johnston-Tyler, MA
EvoLibri Consulting

Printed in the United States of America

First Printing, July 2018

ISBN-13: 978-1723170591
ISBN-10: 1723170593

EvoLibri Consulting
www.evolibri.com
info@evolibri.com

Cover Design, Graphics, and Typesetting by Jan Johnston-Tyler
Edited by Utana Baxter
Final Bookbuilding by Richard Coda Design, LLC

People never grow up. They just learn how to act in public.

— Bryan White, Author

TABLE OF CONTENTS

IN THE KITCHEN

ORGANIZATION

BEING WELL

PERSONAL FINANCES

HOME SWEET HOME

HAVING FUN

LifeLaunch
Student's Handbook

About this Training Course
Welcome to LifeLaunch!

This training course was specifically designed to teach you the basic skills you'll need as you head out into the world as a young adult. It doesn't cover everything you'll need to know, but it does cover a lot. We've tried to make it both comprehensive and engaging, but some of that depends on you. We hope that you'll take this opportunity to learn some skills, maybe make some new friends, and up your 'adulting' game to prepare for your next adventures in life.

Who this Course is Intended For

This course was developed specifically for older teens and young adults. We've tried to write it in a way that meets your needs – easy to read, some exercises and quizzes along the way, and skills that you will actually use, now and later in life.

What You Will Learn
Here's a rundown of what you will be learning:

In the Kitchen

❑ **Kitchen Skills Basics**
Kitchen safety; introduction to essential kitchen tools; proper knife and tool use; grocery list and shopping (where and when and what); stocking a pantry and freezer; kitchen cleaning.

❑ **Cooking Basics**
Menu planning and recipe research; cooking methods; clean up; food storage.

❑ **Nutrition Basics**
Food pyramids and exceptions (special diets); Importance of protein rich foods and impact of diet on daily functioning; nutrition basics

Organization

❑ **Organization Basics**
The basics of organization in the home, including setting up a filing system.

❑ **Calendaring and Organizational Basics**
How to use online and cell phone calendars, and how to sync them if possible. Using calendars to remember repeating events (birthdays, anniversaries, car oil changes), and how to get in the habit of putting everything on the calendar.

❑ **Time Management Basics**
Identifying time wasters vs important work, learning how to break down large goals into smaller, 'doable' chunks.

Being Well

❑ **Personal Wellness Basics**
The basics of physical and mental wellness; what to do to maintain and what to do when something goes wrong.

❑ **First Aid and Emergency Preparedness**
Basic first aid; preparing for an emergency and what to do during and after an emergency; keeping lists of important information; who to contact when.

❑ **Personal Safety Basics**
How to stay safe at home, school/office, and when traveling.

Personal Finance Basics

❑ **Budgeting and Paying Bills**
The basics of budgeting, estimating expenses, and how to stay on top of bills each month.

❑ **Different Types of Financial Accounts**
Instruction of the various types of financial accounts, investment instruments, and the importance of good credit.

❑ **Taxes**
The various types of taxes we all pay; what federal and state income taxes are, how they are paid; the different types of employment and how they impact taxes.

Housing and Living Independently

❑ **Housing Options**
Difference between renting, leasing, and owning, and why each makes sense in different circumstances; how to read a rental/lease agreement; how to look for apartments; how to find good roommates and how to be a good roommate.

❑ **Roommates**
How to be a good roommate, and what to do if you are arguing with your roommates. Setting expectations and sticking to them.

❑ **Housekeeping and Home Maintenance Basics**
How to keep a house relatively clean and orderly; how to clean a kitchen, bathroom, general rooms; laundry and ironing; how to make basic home repairs; annual maintenance.

Having Fun

- ❑ **Building a Social Life**
  Activities to try; getting out; fostering friendships; social etiquette.

- ❑ **Dating and Entertaining**
  The basics of dating; small talk, personal hygiene. Hosting and planning events.

- ❑ **Sex**
  The important things to know about intimate relationships, include a section on Sex and the Internet.

- ❑ **Carrying on Traditions**
  Importance of creating your own traditions as an adult.

SECTION 1

IN THE KITCHEN

Nothing to Eat – Pantry Essentials

You're tired. You're cranky. Most importantly, you're hungry. You come home, look through the fridge, nothing. You look in the cupboard, nothing. Freezer, nothing. Why is there never anything to eat around here?

The fact of the matter is, there probably is something to eat, just nothing that appeals to you at that moment. And, if there's nothing good to eat, then it means that you don't know how to stock your kitchen pantry so that there is always something fast, easy, and tasty ready to be made.

Let's look at what is in a well-stocked pantry.

Essentials – These are the items that you should always have on hand:

- ❑ Cooking and salad oils
- ❑ Vinegar (red wine and apple cider)
- ❑ All-purpose flour
- ❑ Baking powder and baking soda
- ❑ Condiments (ketchup, mustard, pickles)
- ❑ Coffee and/or tea
- ❑ Dry pasta (preferably whole wheat)
- ❑ Canned beans (refried and/or kidney)
- ❑ Parmesan cheese
- ❑ Potatoes

- ❑ Butter or margarine
- ❑ Sugar, granulated and brown
- ❑ Salad dressing (2 kinds)
- ❑ Dry pancake mix
- ❑ Spices and herbs, flavorings (vanilla), salt and pepper
- ❑ Peanut butter and jam/jelly/honey
- ❑ Rice (white and brown)
- ❑ Onions and garlic
- ❑ Bouillon cubes
- ❑ Canned tomatoes, tomato sauce, and tomato paste

Weekly Items – Purchased every week:

- ❑ Fresh vegetables for steaming and salads
- ❑ Fresh meat, chicken, fish
- ❑ Eggs

- ❑ Fresh fruits
- ❑ Milk or substitute
- ❑ Breads

Healthy Snacks – Quick things to satisfy your appetite:

- ❑ Crackers (whole grain)
- ❑ Cheese (harder cheeses)
- ❑ Yogurt
- ❑ Dried fruits
- ❑ Pita and sliced bread
- ❑ Frozen fruit bars

- ❑ Cold and hot cereals
- ❑ Sliced/deli meats
- ❑ Power bars
- ❑ Nuts
- ❑ Popcorn

Fast Meals – When you're too busy to cook (no more than 2x a week!):

- ❑ Boxed or frozen macaroni and cheese
- ❑ Canned soups (preferably low sodium/ low fat; plus cream of mushroom)
- ❑ Frozen vegetables
- ❑ Flash frozen meatballs
- ❑ Individually-wrapped hamburgers
- ❑ Individually-wrapped frozen chicken breasts
- ❑ Fish sticks or fish filets
- ❑ Frozen dinners (low fat/low sodium)

Fancy Flourishes – Little extras to give your meals a bit more personality:

- ❑ Sour cream or Greek-style yogurt (for potatoes, dips, etc.)
- ❑ Chocolate chips
- ❑ Stir-fry sauce and marinades
- ❑ Croutons
- ❑ Chocolate sauce
- ❑ Boxed cake/brownie mix, canned frosting
- ❑ BBQ sauce
- ❑ Soy sauce
- ❑ Nuts, dried fruits
- ❑ Canned whipped cream (low fat) or frozen non-dairy whipped topping

EXERCISE 1 — CHECK ESSENTIALS AND WEEKLY NEEDS

Shopping is time-consuming and when you're cooking a meal, it is really annoying to find out you are missing a key ingredient. So, plan ahead by planning out meals you intend to make, put those ingredients on the list, but also check your pantry items!

1. Using the list above, go through your pantry to see what items you are missing and think you need. Put them on your list!

2. Make a list every time you shop! You can keep a running shopping list on your cell phone.

3. Shop for pantry items AND ingredients for meals you have planned.

4. If you live with other people, post a list online or on the fridge, and make sure everyone puts used up items on the list.

Try it with this sample shopping list. What would you put on it if you had to go shopping today?

❑ _____   ❑ _____

❑ _____   ❑ _____

❑ _____   ❑ _____

❑ _____   ❑ _____

❑ _____   ❑ _____

❑ _____   ❑ _____

❑ _____   ❑ _____

❑ _____   ❑ _____

❑ _____   ❑ _____

Where's That Pan? – Kitchen Essentials

The next key to being able to prepare fast, nutritious and tasty meals and snacks is having the proper cooking gear. While I was a professional chef for ten years, I don't expect that everyone will have the extensive cooking equipment I have, but there are several pieces that you will need to get going.

Preparation

❑ Good 10" chef knife
❑ Set of metal nesting bowls
❑ Plastic chopping board
❑ 2 wooden spoons
❑ Balloon whisk
❑ Measuring spoons
❑ Metal ladles, large and medium

❑ Good 3" or 4" paring knife
❑ 16" and 12" tongs
❑ Box grater
❑ 2 plastic scrapers
❑ Measuring cups, wet and dry
❑ Metal spatula

Cooking

❑ 8" non-stick fry pan
❑ 1.5-2 qt saucepan
❑ 8 qt stockpot with steamer insert

❑ 12"-16" non-stick fry pan
❑ 4 qt saucepan

Baking

❑ 3 qt oblong Pyrex casserole dish
❑ 1.5 qt round Pyrex casserole dish with cover

❑ 1 9" non-stick pie pan (optional)
❑ 2 non-stick jelly roll type cookie sheets

- ❏ 1.5 qt square Pyrex casserole dish
- ❏ 2 9" round non-stick cake pans (optional)
- ❏ 1 non-stick muffin pan (optional)

Serving

- ❏ Large salad bowl with individual salad bowls
- ❏ 2 serving bowls (small and medium)
- ❏ Salad tongs/servers (optional, can use tongs)
- ❏ 2 serving platters (small and medium)
- ❏ 2 –metal serving spoons

Storage

- ❏ Ziploc baggies
- ❏ Saran Wrap
- ❏ Foil
- ❏ Set of plastic storage ware

EXERCISE 2 — WHAT ELSE DO I NEED?

Take the time to go through your kitchen with the lists above and find out what you have and what you might need now and in the future. You won't need everything right away, but do keep what you're missing in mind as you starting cooking and baking beyond the essentials. Like with your food shopping list, keep a running list on your cell phone, or on Amazon, as things to ask for gifts!

Go through your kitchen and see if there is anything you would add to your 'kitchen wish list'.

❏ _____	❏ _____
❏ _____	❏ _____
❏ _____	❏ _____
❏ _____	❏ _____
❏ _____	❏ _____
❏ _____	❏ _____
❏ _____	❏ _____
❏ _____	❏ _____
❏ _____	❏ _____
❏ _____	❏ _____
❏ _____	❏ _____

Kitchen Safety

Heat and Electricity

❑ Make sure all wires, cords and plugs on your appliances are not frayed and that the plugs have 3-prong grounded connections. This would include coffee makers, toasters, blenders, microwaves, mixers, etc.

❑ Don't leave the kitchen with food cooking on the stove. Turn off burners as soon as you take the pot off.

❑ Avoid wearing loose sleeves and sweaters that can easily catch fire when cooking.

❑ Keep a fire extinguisher in or near the kitchen, but not near the stove or the cooktop.

❑ Scalding is one of the most common injuries in the kitchen. Turn pot handles away from the front of the stove.

❑ Never stick a fork in a toaster to retrieve trapped toast – you may get shocking results!

❑ Microwave cooking is fast but can cause serious burns. Check with a teacher for specific directions before using the microwave oven. Use only microwave-safe cookware.

❑ Food coming out of the microwave can be very hot. Allow the food to cool for several minutes before eating. This includes popcorn! Steam from the bag can cause serious burns.

❑ Keep a good selection of hot pads and oven mitts on hand. Always use them for any item that has been heated in any way, especially items coming out of the microwave, over or toaster oven.

❑ Steam can burn just as easily as boiling liquid or a hot burner. Always keep your face and hands away from rising steam.

❑ Keep wet hands away from electrical outlets.

EXERCISE 3 — QUICK KITCHEN SAFETY SURVEY

Using the list above, go through your kitchen area and check to make sure that your kitchen appliance cords aren't frayed, that you have a fire extinguisher (and know how to use it!) and that you have ample thick hotpads available when cooking.

Review the rest of the safety tips and discuss with a parent at home. What other dangers are present? Trip hazards? Broken appliances? List any potential hazards here:

❑ _____   ❑ _____

❑ _____   ❑ _____

❑ _____   ❑ _____

❑ _____   ❑ _____

❑ _____   ❑ _____

❑ _____   ❑ _____

❑ _____   ❑ _____

❑ _____   ❑ _____

❑ _____   ❑ _____

❑ _____   ❑ _____

Handling Knives and Sharp Objects

❑ Keep blades sharp and handles clean.

❑ Always cut away from your body when using a knife.

❑ Always hold food you are cutting with your fingers curled under, not with fingers flat over food.

❑ Always use a cutting board.

❑ Don't put knives in a sink of soapy water – they may not be seen and accidents can occur. Wash immediately and set to dry on the counter away from the edge and laying flat.

❑ Don't attempt to catch a knife as it falls – JUMP BACK! It is better that it hits the floor than your hand or foot.

Cleanliness and Food Safety

❑ Clean up spills immediately – floors are slippery when wet.

❑ Store cleaning supplies and all chemicals in a safe place and always away from all food. Use safety latches.

❑ Wash your hands before handling food and after handling meat or poultry. Hands can be a virtual freight train of bacteria. Also, carefully wash your cutting board with hot soapy water after using it for poultry, fish, or meat.

❑ Wash all fruits and vegetables before eating. Use just clear, clean water, no soap.

❑ Discard or compost foods like bread, cheese, jelly, fruits, vegetables or any other foods that have mold spots or look bad. Fruits and vegetables that are shriveled or have soft spots should be thrown away or composted.

EXERCISE 4 — FOOD SAFETY QUIZ

1. **List three important safety techniques when handling knives.**
   - ☐ Handshake hold
   - ☐ Don't put the knife in a soapy sink.
   - ☐ When dropping a knife, let it drop.

2. **If food is soft, has mold, or looks suspicious, what should you do?**
   Compost it.

3. **When should you wash your hands?**
   - Every time when you want to handle food.
   - After touching raw meat.

4. **How should you clean fruit and vegetables?**
   Wash the surface

5. **How often should you wash your cutting board?**
   Wash it after you cut your food.

General Cleaning Tips

Have a place for everything. It's much easier to use a utensil or appliance, clean it and put it away when it has a home. For example, I have a special drawer that is used just for foil, plastic wrap and parchment paper. Those items are always easy to find, and are put away after each use because they have a special home. Here are more tips and tricks. Read and learn!

→ **Never mix ammonia and bleach because it will create toxic fumes!**

❑ Always, always, always clean as you go. Rinse bowls and knives that don't need complete washing, put ingredients away as you use them, wipe down messes the minute you make them.

❑ Identify spots in your kitchen that accumulate clutter and take a few minutes every day (or at least once a week) to clear those spots and place objects in their correct homes.

❑ Try to end each day with a clean, empty kitchen sink. Run the dishwasher before you go to bed and unload it first thing in the morning.

❑ A sponge is actually a great way to spread germs. I prefer using paper towels, discarding them after cleaning each surface, to totally prevent cross-contamination.

❑ To quickly clean burned food on a pan, add some dish soap and 1/2" of water. Bring to a boil, then let the liquid cool in the pan. The burned food will be easy to remove.

❑ When food spills over and burns on the oven floor, sprinkle a handful of salt on the mess. The smoke will be reduced and the spill easier to clean after the oven cools. You can add some cinnamon to the salt to help reduce odors.

❑ To clean your microwave oven, mix together 2 Tbsp. of lemon juice or vinegar and 2 cups of water in a 4 cup glass microwave safe bowl. Microwave on HIGH for two to three minutes. Carefully remove the bowl and wipe the microwave with paper towels. Repeat as necessary.

❑ Try putting lemon or lime pieces through the garbage disposal every few days for a clean fresh smell. To freshen the garbage disposal, sprinkle a couple of tablespoons of baking soda down the drain, drop in two ice cubes and turn it on. Then run the hot water for a few minutes while the disposal is working.

❑ Clean your coffee maker every few weeks by filling the water reservoir with equal parts white vinegar and water and putting it through the brew cycle. Then use clean fresh water and repeat the brew cycle to rinse the machine. Repeat with fresh water two more times.

❑ If you don't have a self-cleaning oven, scrape up any large spills, then spray cleaner inside the oven, close the door and let it sit overnight so the cleaner has time to work.

❏ For glass cooktops, there are special commercial cleaners that work well. Use them with a hard plastic scraper to remove burned-on food. Clean your glass cooktop as soon as it cools to avoid having to scrub burned food.

❏ To clean a blender, squirt a few drops of liquid soap into it, fill halfway with warm water, cover and blend away the mess. Rinse and repeat if necessary. You can also use this method for food processors.

❏ For lime and mineral deposits on your kitchen sink faucet, wrap vinegar-soaked paper towels around faucets for about an hour. This breaks down the mineral scale, and the chrome will be clean and shiny after buffing with a dry paper towel.

❏ If you don't have a self-cleaning oven, place racks in the bathtub with about 1/2 cup dishwasher detergent and cover them with several inches of warm water. Let the racks soak for 45 minutes, then rinse and dry.

EXERCISE 5 — CLEANING REVIEW

List five 'best practices' that you can use right away to help keep your kitchen clean:

1.

2.

3.

4.

5.

Meal Planning

Planning for the Week

One skill you need to develop is to try to plan meals – even generally – a week in advance. This doesn't have to be very structured, unless you want it to be (and some people do). Even if you all you do is to make sure that you buy 3-4 cuts of fresh meat, fish, and poultry and have several fast meals you can make (fish sticks, meatballs, etc.), along with adequate veggies, fruits, dairy, and sides (potatoes, pasta, rice), you can make an easy dinner every night.

Another skill to develop is to cook 'big things' on the weekend when you have more time. For example, you can roast a whole chicken on Sunday night, and then use the leftovers for chicken quesadillas, chicken sandwiches, and chicken noodle casserole later in the week.

Here's a visual chart for learning how to 'think' a week in advance when you go shopping:

On...	I'll make...	Because...
Sunday	Roast chicken	I have time to cook on Sunday
Monday	Fish sticks (from freezer)	I have a late class, and am tired on Mondays
Tuesday	Pork Chops	It's my regular schedule
Wednesday	Stir-fry	I have lots of time on Wednesdays to cook
Thursday	Chicken quesadillas with leftover chicken	I have a late class, and I come home tired
Friday	Nothing	I'm going out to dinner
Saturday	Pizza	Friends come over, make pizza

EXERCISE 6 — MAPPING OUT YOUR COOKING WEEK

Your turn! Map out the coming week in the same way.

On...	I'll make...	Because...
Sunday		
Monday		
Tuesday		
Wednesday		
Thursday		
Friday		
Saturday		

Finding and Reading Recipes

Cooking can be more fun if you try new things, and it's easy to find recipes and experiment a bit. Not only can you find recipes in cookbooks, but the internet has lots of resources you can use. Some of my favorites include:

- ❑ www.epicurious.com

- ❑ www.allrecipes.com

- ❑ www.foodnetwork.com

- ❑ www.cookinglight.com

Most of these websites have special features, such as a 'virtual' recipe file where you can store recipes you've used, or search engines that allow you to search for recipes based on a food you have in the fridge (like, kumquats, or chicken, or horseradish!).

Reading recipes is fairly easy – just think of it as a science project. Here are the steps:

1. Always read the recipe completely through before you begin:

   □ Do you have all of the ingredients you need?

   □ Do you have all of the equipment you need?

   □ Do you have enough time to complete the recipe, including any time that it will take you to prepare the recipe AND cook it?

   □ Assemble all of the ingredients on the kitchen counter.

   □ Assemble all of the equipment on the counter.

2. Re-read the recipe:

   □ Do you need to heat the oven?

   □ Do you need to separate eggs, or beat them, or sift flour, trim meat? Do that now!

3. Follow the directions in the recipe. Once you are a good cook, you can start improvising, but when you are just starting out, follow the recipe!

4. As you are preparing the recipe, try to keep the kitchen clean and uncluttered:

   □ Rinse bowls and measuring cups and either put them in the sink or better yet, straight into the dishwasher unless you'll need them again.

   □ Put food away (eggs, milk, flour, etc.) after you use it.

5. Keep referring back to the recipe at each step to ensure that you don't miss something.

6. While the dish is cooking, take the time to put things in the dishwasher, wash them by hand if necessary, and wipe off the counter.

7. When the meal is done, sit down and enjoy!

EXERCISE 7— RESEARCH FIVE RECIPES TO TRY

1. Take a look at your plan to cook for the week. Do you need any recipes? Main dishes, side dishes, desserts?

2. Check out the various recipe websites listed, and see if you prefer one over the other. List one you like best.

3. Look up five recipes you are willing to try, and use the 'save' features on those websites so you can easily find the recipes later. List them here:

    ❑ _____

    ❑ _____

    ❑ _____

    ❑ _____

    ❑ _____

4. Remember that cooking and baking are a little like science experiments where you learn as you go. You can make notes, try recipes, and even get creative over time. Try new things!

Cooking Basics

Before we get started on cooking, we need to introduce some terms and techniques. You don't need to memorize or learn everything we go over here, but it's a good idea to get some exposure to the various types of cooking you may encounter.

General Cooking Terms

We're going to learn how to do many of these, but first let's see how many of these terms and methods you know already:

- ❑ <u>Bake</u> — To cook in an oven
- ❑ <u>Beat</u> — To mix ingredients together using a fast, circular movement with a spoon, fork, whisk or mixer
- ❑ <u>Blend</u> —To mix ingredients together gently with a spoon, fork, or until combined
- ❑ <u>Boil</u> —To heat a food so that the liquid gets hot enough for bubbles to rise and break the surface
- ❑ <u>Broil</u> —To cook under direct heat
- ❑ <u>Brown</u> —To cook over medium or high heat until surface of food browns or darkens
- ❑ <u>Drain</u> —To remove all the liquid using a colander, strainer, or by pressing a plate against the food while tilting the container
- ❑ <u>Grease</u> —To lightly coat with oil, butter, margarine, or non-stick spray so food does not stick when cooking or baking
- ❑ <u>Knead</u> —To press, fold and stretch dough until it is smooth and uniform, usually done by pressing with the heels of the hands
- ❑ <u>Marinate</u> —To soak food in a liquid to tenderize or add flavor to it (the liquid is called a "marinade")
- ❑ <u>Mash</u> —To squash food with a fork, spoon, or masher
- ❑ <u>Mix</u> —To stir ingredients together with a spoon, fork, or electric mixer until combined
- ❑ <u>Preheat</u> —To turn oven on ahead of time so that it is at the desired temperature when needed (usually takes about 5 to 10 minutes)
- ❑ <u>Sauté</u> —To cook quickly in a little oil, butter, or margarine
- ❑ <u>Simmer</u> —To cook in liquid over low heat (low boil) so that bubbles just begin to break the surface
- ❑ <u>Steam</u> —To cook food over steam without putting the food directly in water (usually done with a steamer)

❏ <u>Sweat</u> — To cook high-moisture food in a low heat, dry (or nearly dry) pan to cook in own moisture

❏ <u>Stir Fry</u> —To quickly cook small pieces of food over high heat while constantly stirring the food until it is crisply tender (usually done with a wok)

EXERCISE 8 — COOKING METHODS QUIZ

Without looking at the list, name six methods of preparing food:

1.

2.

3.

4.

5.

6.

Knife Techniques

Using a knife properly is a very important part of most cooking. We mentioned earlier that you should have a quality knife and it should be sharp at all times. If you have a dull knife, you can either learn how to sharpen it yourself, or you can take it in to a professional for sharpening.

These instructions are not meant to replace hands-on training. For more information on technique, you can watch any of the number of cooking shows, or watch YouTube videos for more information. Really work on your knife techniques. Impress your friends and neighbors!

❏ <u>Slice</u> — Slicing is the basis for most knife techniques:

▫ Hold the object to be cut in your non-dominant hand, with your fingers curled under (not flattened out over the object).

▫ Press down on the object to hold it in place.

▫ Hold the knife in your dominant hand, gripping it tightly.

▫ With a 'push and saw' motion, cut into the food —the blade of the knife should be parallel to your knuckles.

- Press down to the cutting board, lift and repeat.

❑ <u>Chop</u> —To cut into small pieces. Typically, you will start by slicing the food into thin strips, and then cutting them in the opposite way to form a chop. Pieces can be irregular in shape.

❑ <u>Dice</u> —To cut into small cubes. Again, you'll typically start by slicing the food into strips and then carefully cutting them into cubes or 'dice'. Small dice should be about 1/8 of an inch, and a large dice should be approximately 3/4 of an inch. Pieces should be regular in shape. Note that this is typically only used with foods that are eaten raw (apples) or will hold their shape after cooking.

❑ <u>Julienne</u> — To cut into thin strips, as above, but without cutting into a dice. Pieces should be regular in shape.

❑ <u>Grate or Shred</u> — To use a grater to make thin pieces. Shredded food usually is not cut with a knife but is passed over the surface of a grater. You can get a similar effect by carefully shaving food with a sharp knife.

❑ <u>Mince</u> —To cut into very small pieces, smaller than chopped or diced pieces. Mincing is cut into such fine pieces that the food is nearly pulverized. This is done when you don't want to eat a large chunk of something, like raw garlic.

EXERCISE 9 — KNIFE PRACTICE

Everyone should have two Russet potatoes to practice with.

1. **First, start by slicing one of the potatoes, both in thick and thin slices. Remember to curl your fingers under when holding the potato!**

2. **Take the larger slices and cut them into a dice. Take some of the thinner slices, and cut them into julienne/strips.**

3. **Take some of the juliennes and first chop, then mince them.**

4. **Practice again with the second potato.**

Cooking Techniques

Next, we'll look at cooking techniques. There's a lot to learn, so don't worry about getting it all down right away.

Dry Heat Cooking Methods

The first of the two major categories in cooking methods is dry heat where no liquid is added to the food for cooking.

- ❑ Baking —If you are putting food into a closed, heated box of some sort, you are baking, particularly if the food is a prepared mixture of some sort (casseroles, cookies, bread).

- ❑ Roasting — Roasting typically refers to 'baking' a whole food such as meats, fish, game, or vegetables. Roasting typically caramelize the skin to a deep brown, but keeps the interior of the food moist.

- ❑ Broiling —Foods are typically broiled in an oven where the heat comes from the top of the unit, rather than the bottom. This technique is used to quickly crisp or brown foods that will overcook if baked at a lower temperature.

- ❑ Grilling or Barbecue —Grilled foods are cooked either over a flame or on a specialized pan or grate to impart grilling marks and deep flavor. When cooked outside on a BBQ using briquets or woods, the grilling has an addition of smoky flavors.

- ❑ Pan Frying —Pan frying uses a small amount of fat to keep the food from sticking to while cooking over high heat. This technique is good for getting a deep-brown crust on high-moisture foods.

- ❑ Sautéing —Sautéing is similar to pan frying, but typically uses a lower temperature. The end result is not deep brown but translucent or light brown.

- ❑ Sweating —Sweating involves a small amount of fat or moisture, and covering the pan to allow the food to 'sweat' until cooked. The food does not brown. This technique is used in high moisture foods like asparagus and spinach.

- ❑ Deep Frying —Deep Frying is immersion of foods in hot oil until they are thoroughly cooked and golden brown. →This technique is potentially dangerous, and should only be undertaken with guidance, or by a competent cook with a fire extinguisher nearby!

- ❑ Flambé/Torching —Fun with fire! Some recipes call for adding liquor to sauté pans, which flares up quickly, and burns off the alcohol, which is called flambé. Using a kitchen torch imparts a brown crust on delicate foods, such as creme caramel.
  → These techniques are potentially dangerous and should only be used with supervision.

Moist Heat Cooking Methods

The second of the two major categories in cooking methods is the moist heat collection of methods. Moist heat refers to the use of water, liquid or steam in these cooking methods. These methods are mostly distinguished by the temperature of the water; a few of them also stipulate the amount of water or liquid used.

❑ <u>Blanch</u> —Blanching is a 'quick plunge' of delicate food into hot water, and then quickly removing the food and cooling it with ice water or in the refrigerator. This is done to quickly cook foods but keep them crisp, such as green beans or asparagus for a cold salad.

❑ <u>Boil</u> —Boiling is cooking in, well, boiling water or other liquid. This is done to quickly rehydrate or break down a food such as dry pasta or tomatoes for a tomato sauce.

❑ <u>Braise</u> —Braising is amazing. Braising typically cooks meats and vegetables in flavorful liquids, at a relatively low temperature. Think stews, soups, pot roasts, pulled pork. This can be done either on the stove or in the oven. And the pot should be covered to keep in those luscious flavors.

❑ <u>Poach</u> —Similar to braising, poaching cooks foods surrounded by liquid, but at a very low temperature and typically for a short period of time. Eggs and soft fruits such as pears are typically poached.

❑ <u>Simmer</u> —Simmering is also similar to braising, but typically we want to 'reduce' the water content in the dish (making stock, for example) so the lid is typically left off. Temperature is low, and typically foods are cooked for a long while, 30 minutes or more, to fully mingle flavors.

❑ <u>Steam</u> —Steaming is a useful way to cook delicate foods and to ensure that they retain their nutritional content by suspending the food above boiling or simmering water, and allowing the rising steam to cook the food. This also is an excellent way to cook fish.

List six ways of cooking from the above lists that you will try in the next few weeks, along with the food you will cook:

1.

2.

3.

4.

5.

Additional Cooking Tips

Everyone can cook well with a little practice, and with a little help. Here are some additional tips for cooking.

1. Don't go too cheap on your ingredients. It's better to have a smaller portion of a really good piece of beef and supplement with side dishes than to eat a large, and very tough, steak. Cheap Parmesan cheese has fillers such as corn meal which don't add flavor, so use a better type of parm on your dishes.

2. Don't be afraid to use your hands when cooking, so long as they are clean. Your hands are often the best way to mix ingredients, pat food into a pan, or crumble herbs.

3. Use kosher or sea salt when seasoning food. It has better flavor.

4. Don't be in a hurry when you're cooking or baking. If you need to cook two batches of food rather than to cram everything into one pan, do that.

5. Food continues to cook after removing it from the flame or the oven. It's better to take something out too soon than too late. You can always pop something back in a pan, but if it's overcooked, yuck.

6. Roasted meats need to rest on the counter before carving for at least five minutes so that the liquids reabsorb into the meat.

7. Use a timer and a thermometer for cooking and baking. You don't want to know that dinner is 'done' when the smoke detector goes off!

How to Shop

There are a couple of tricks to shopping cost- and time-effectively:

- ❑ First off, try to never shop when you are hungry. It's human nature to throw a bunch of high-fat foods in your shopping cart when you're hungry, so try to avoid it.

- ❑ The next trick is to try to shop for your weekly items only once or twice a week. If you find that you are going to the grocery store for your essentials more frequently, it means that you are not planning ahead. With the cost of gas these days, it is very much worth the time to sit and write up a grocery list before you leave the house.

- ❑ If you can, try to shop at non-peak periods (like, weekends and evenings). The middle of a weekday is usually a good time, as the shelves and produce tends to be well-stocked, and there aren't a lot of other shoppers.

- ❑ When possible, try to shop for your essentials only once or twice a month. You may run out of an item in between, and that's fine, but with a bit of planning, you can avoid lots of trips. The upside of this planning also means that you will have good, nutritious foods on hand at all times.

- ❑ Also, try to be good to the environment, and either recycle paper/plastic bags, or purchase shopping bags to reuse on shopping trips.

- ❑ Learn where to buy which items. While you may spend a bit more on gas to get between stores, you will save money over the long term by choosing the store based on what you are buying.

- ❑ Try to plan your shopping trips so that you can run errands or do more than one type of shopping without going out of your way.

EXERCISE 11 — SHOPPING QUIZ

1. **When is a good time to go shopping?**

2. **When shouldn't you shop?**

3. **How often should you plan on shopping?**

4. **What should you remember to take when you go shopping?**

Shopping Tricks

Believe it or not, there is a science behind grocery store layout and product placement, and it's all around getting you to buy things you don't need and to spend more money. Shocking, right?

Once in the grocery store, here are some additional tricks to know:

❑ Most common items are mid-level on shelves. More expensive items are typically higher, and cheaper items (bulk, store brand) are typically lower.

❑ Dairy, bread and meat items are typically at the back of the store, as a way of making you walk through the aisles to get to them in an effort to make you pick things up on the way.

❑ End caps at the front of the store (the end of each aisle) are a retailer's dream. It's the place where they can catch your attention easily to get you to buy things they want to move quickly, or are on special. Halloween candy, Budweiser, Coca-Cola products may all end up there. End caps at the back of the store are typically reserved for one type of product (tortillas) or one very popular brand (Campbell soups).

❑ When buying fresh fruits and veggies, make sure to check the back of the pile if the items in the front look dinged-up or are over-ripe. Test by gently pressing food. Very slight resistance means 'ready to eat'. Super soft means 'beyond it's prime'.

❑ Make sure that veggies and fruit are bright and colorful, with no brown spots.

Where Should I Shop?

Depending on what you need to shop for, there are several places where you can do your grocery shopping and even save money.

1. Discount Stores (Grocery Outlet, Costco, Smart & Final): for cleaning supplies, paper goods, aluminum foil, Saran wrap, baggies, light bulbs, pet food, charcoal, frozen food, some fresh foods, cheese, food for parties/large gatherings, sodas and bottled water

2. Farmers' Markets: Compare prices with Trader Joe's/supermarkets to see if you are getting a better deal. You may have to pay higher, but the quality could be better.

3. Trader Joe's: for fresh fruits, veggies, meats, dairy, fish, breads, cereal, rice, pasta (whole wheat), soups, canned tomatoes, frozen veggies, lunch meats, condiments, etc.

4. Grocery Stores (Safeway, Lucky, Nob Hill): for specialty and name-brand items, if you can't find them elsewhere.

EXERCISE 12 — SHOPPING TRICKS

List six tricks you've learned about shopping below:

1.

2.

3.

4.

5.

6.

Nutrition

Why is cooking and shopping important? Because food is our fuel, and just like all complex 'machines', what we put into our bodies determines how well we 'run'.

There are three main aspects to nutrition:

1. Nutrients to regenerate and fuel our bodies

2. Fiber and water we need for digestion

3. Calories so that we can maintain an ideal weight

Nutrients

At a molecular level, our bodies need many nutrients to perform the tasks we ask of them, and without these nutrients we cannot function:

❏ <u>Protein</u> —Protein is found in many foods, but is richest in animal products (meat, cheese), beans and legumes, and some grains.

❏ <u>Fats</u> — Fats or oils are also found in many foods, and while some fat is essential to health, too much causes unnecessary weight gain.

❏ <u>Carbohydrates</u> —Carbs are necessary for generating energy in our bodies, but too many, again, can cause unnecessary weight gain. In general, carbs should be in the form of whole grains, whole vegetables and fruits, and not from processed food.

❏ <u>Vitamins and Minerals</u> — Also referred to as micronutrients, vitamins and minerals are in many of the foods we eat, and to get all of the vitamins and minerals we need, we should eat a diverse array of foods. Vitamin and mineral deficiencies can be extremely dangerous and cause a wide range of health problems.

Fiber and Water

Many of us do not drink enough water, which is the primary way we flush our bodies of built-up toxins and materials we don't need in our system anymore. Drinking plenty of fluids during the day is essential to our health, and failure to do so can cause us to get headaches, muscle cramps, or dizziness.

Fiber is also an important aid to digestion, as we need bulk to 'sweep away' all the crud that builds up in our systems. Inadequate amounts of either water or fiber will cause you to become constipated – enough said and a good reason to eat whole grains, whole fruits, and whole vegetables!

Calorie Intake

Probably the trickiest part of nutrition for Americans isn't so much getting enough of what they need, but not getting too much of what they don't need – calories.

Most nutritionists and doctors would agree that the best way to gain, lose, or maintain weight is to have a good idea of how many calories you are putting into your body each day. While you don't have to count calories every day for the rest of your life, it is a very good idea, once in a while, to track your caloric intake for a few days and see how you are faring.

An average woman needs about 1800-2000 calories a day, and an average man needs about 2200-2400 a day. These averages depend greatly on activity level (how much you exercise), age (the older we get the less calories we need), genetics (some of us have faster metabolisms), and current height and weight (taller/larger people may need more calories to maintain their current weight).

EXERCISE 13 — NUTRITION QUIZ

1. **What are the three main aspects of nutrition?**

   ☐ _Nutrients_
   ☐ _Fiber and water_
   ☐ _Calorie intake_

2. **What are four main sources of nutrients?**

   ☐ _Protein_
   ☐ _Fat_
   ☐ _Carbohydrates_
   ☐ _Vitamins and Minerals_

3. **What can be tricky about calories?**

   Eating too much.

4. **How many calories should the average man consume each day?**

   Man: 2200 - 2400
   Woman: 18 - 2000

Nutrition Guidelines

While there is some controversy over exactly how much of each food group healthy people normally should consume, the USDA's chart is a good basis for understanding the types and amounts of different foods most adults should eat.

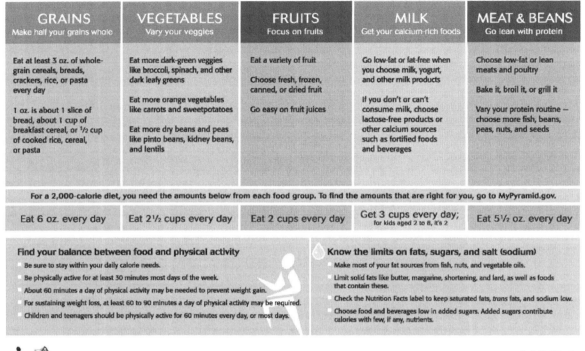

GRAINS Make half your grains whole	VEGETABLES Vary your veggies	FRUITS Focus on fruits	MILK Get your calcium-rich foods	MEAT & BEANS Go lean with protein
Eat at least 3 oz. of whole-grain cereals, breads, crackers, rice, or pasta every day 1 oz. is about 1 slice of bread, about 1 cup of breakfast cereal, or ½ cup of cooked rice, cereal, or pasta	Eat more dark-green veggies like broccoli, spinach, and other dark leafy greens Eat more orange vegetables like carrots and sweetpotatoes Eat more dry beans and peas like pinto beans, kidney beans, and lentils	Eat a variety of fruit Choose fresh, frozen, canned, or dried fruit Go easy on fruit juices	Go low-fat or fat-free when you choose milk, yogurt, and other milk products If you don't or can't consume milk, choose lactose-free products or other calcium sources such as fortified foods and beverages	Choose low-fat or lean meats and poultry Bake it, broil it, or grill it Vary your protein routine — choose more fish, beans, peas, nuts, and seeds

For a 2,000-calorie diet, you need the amounts below from each food group. To find the amounts that are right for you, go to MyPyramid.gov.

Eat 6 oz. every day	Eat 2½ cups every day	Eat 2 cups every day	Get 3 cups every day; for kids aged 2 to 8, it's 2	Eat 5½ oz. every day

Find your balance between food and physical activity
- Be sure to stay within your daily calorie needs.
- Be physically active for at least 30 minutes most days of the week.
- About 60 minutes a day of physical activity may be needed to prevent weight gain.
- For sustaining weight loss, at least 60 to 90 minutes a day of physical activity may be required.
- Children and teenagers should be physically active for 60 minutes every day, or most days.

Know the limits on fats, sugars, and salt (sodium)
- Make most of your fat sources from fish, nuts, and vegetable oils.
- Limit solid fats like butter, margarine, shortening, and lard, as well as foods that contain these.
- Check the Nutrition Facts label to keep saturated fats, trans fats, and sodium low.
- Choose food and beverages low in added sugars. Added sugars contribute calories with few, if any, nutrients.

MyPyramid.gov
STEPS TO A HEALTHIER YOU

U.S. Department of Agriculture
Center for Nutrition Policy and Promotion
April 2005
CNPP-15

Charting Your Foods

On the next page you will find the USDA's MyPyramid Worksheet. This is a good way to map out the foods you will eat over a period of time so that you can ensure that you are getting the right nutrients, getting exercise, and keeping your calories within normal ranges.

Remember that what is right for you may not be right for everyone else, so work with your teacher, parents, or a nutritionist to determine what will be the best balanced diet for you.

MyPyramid Worksheet

Check how you did today and set a goal to aim for tomorrow

MyPyramid.gov
STEPS TO A HEALTHIER YOU

Food Group	Tip	Goal Based on a 1400 calorie pattern.	List each food choice in its food group*	Estimate Your Total
GRAINS	Make at least half your grains whole grains	**5 ounce equivalents** (1 ounce equivalent is about 1 slice bread, 1 cup dry cereal, or ½ cup cooked rice, pasta, or cereal)		___ ounce equivalents
VEGETABLES	Try to have vegetables from several subgroups each day	**1 ½ cups** Subgroups: Dark Green, Orange, Starchy, Dry Beans and Peas, Other Veggies		___ cups
FRUITS	Make most choices fruit, not juice	**1 ½ cups**		___ cups
MILK	Choose fat-free or low fat most often	**2 cups** (1 ½ ounces cheese = 1 cup milk)		___ cups
MEAT & BEANS	Choose lean meat and poultry. Vary your choices—more fish, beans, peas, nuts, and seeds	**4 ounce equivalents** (1 ounce equivalent is 1 ounce meat, poultry, or fish, 1 egg, 1 T. peanut butter, ½ ounce nuts, or ¼ cup dry beans)		___ ounce equivalents
PHYSICAL ACTIVITY	Build more physical activity into your daily routine at home and work.	At least **30 minutes** of moderate to vigorous activity a day, 10 minutes or more at a time.	*Some foods don't fit into any group. These "extras" may be mainly fat or sugar— limit your intake of these.	___ minutes

Write in Your Choices for Today

31

Reading Labels

Below is a sample label from the USDA for a serving of mac and cheese. Note that important facts to pay attention to are serving size (usually much smaller than we would typically eat), fat and sugars in the item, and whether or not there is much protein, fiber, or vitamins and minerals in the product. Is it actually good for us?

EXERCISE 14 — LABEL QUIZ

1. **Why read labels?**

2. **How can labels be misleading?**

    It depends on th the serving size

3. **What are three important things to look for on a label?**

    Total fat, Carbohydrates, protein

4. **Will knowing this information help you make different choices when shopping? How so?**

SECTION 2

ORGANIZATION

Why Be Organized?

Believe it or not, being somewhat organized makes life much easier. And conversely, being disorganized makes life hard. While I don't encourage my clients to become OCD, I do encourage them to find ways that work for them to keep their lives running smoothly. Here are some basics to get started:

❑ **Calendaring** – Keeping an up-to-date calendar with all of your important meetings, to-do items, and tasks helps ensure that you don't forget where you are supposed to be, and don't forget to do important things like refill your meds, pay your insurance, or take care of your pets. It also helps you to plan ahead, as you'll see below.

❑ **Planning Ahead** – Using a calendar to look ahead helps in many ways. It helps you focus on the important things coming up so you don't feel overwhelmed at the last moment. It helps you save time by being able to group your chores and errands (cleaning both the bathroom and the kitchen because friends are coming over; going to get gas the night before an appointment, because you'll be going the opposite way). When you know what is coming up in the next few days you can take action now, rather than waiting until the last minute and feeling overwhelmed.

❑ **Same Place Every Time** – Lots of people have a hard time remembering where they put their keys, or where they last put the flashlight, or where they put their credit cards. The best way to remember these things is to always put these things in the same place every time. Can you imagine how hard it would be if you didn't put your clean coffee cups all in the same place, each time you emptied the dishwasher? You'd never find them without opening every cupboard. The same is true for your keys, your wallet, your cell phone, and other items you spend time hunting down. Pick a place for your keys, and always put them there when you walk into the house. Always return your flashlight to the same drawer in the kitchen. Do you always forget to put the flashlight back, because you frequently use it in another room? Buy another flashlight, and put it in that room, and always in the same place. It's easy!

❑ **Cut Down on Hassle** – Whether or not we know it, we all spend time doing a lot of things that we really don't need to be doing, or don't need to do right then and there. Normally, that's okay, but when we are tight on time, we need to recognize what is truly important for us to focus on. For example, while you may like to always answer your phone when it's ringing, if you are trying to finish a gardening project before it is dark, let voicemail get it, and call back when you're done. Try to keep the distractions down, and complete non-essential tasks when you have time.

❑ **Good Habits** – Using your time wisely is sometimes just a matter of forming good habits. For example, if you like to watch TV in the evening, why not use that time to do your laundry? You can start and change loads on commercial breaks, and fold dry laundry while you're watching. This way, you can get work done, get some relaxation in, and feel good about keeping on top of your housework.

❑ **Ten Minute Cleanup** – One way to stay organized is to cut down on clutter and mess. A quick way to do this is to put on your favorite loud, fast music, get a garbage bag, and quickly go from room to room picking up and throwing away trash -- junk mail, newspapers, empty cans, etc. Next, pick up the closest clutter in whatever room you are in. Run to the rooms where that clutter belongs and put it down. Pick up any clutter in THOSE rooms that belongs elsewhere, put things back in their respective rooms as you go from one room to another. Once you have moved everything back to their proper rooms, go to one room at a time, and put everything away.

EXERCISE 1 — ORGANIZING QUIZ

1. In what simple ways can you be more organized, starting today?

2. Why is being a little organized a good idea?

3. How might your life be improved if you followed a few of these organizational tips?

Electronic Calendars

One of the best ways to get and keep yourself organized is to use (faithfully!) an electronic calendar of some sort. The most common applications are Google Calendar, Ical for the Mac and iPhone, and Office365's Outlook for PCs. These are all readily available and work in much the same way. It really is a matter of personal preference as to which one you use. The key here is: USE ONE! Most people cannot function effectively without a calendar, and people with ASD or ADHD have an even more difficult time than most without one.

If you like to write things down in a paper calendar, that's fine too. The challenge is that they are harder to keep up to date, and you may not have it with you when you need it. If you are committed to using a paper calendar, and carry it with you wherever you go, that's fine.

What to Look for in a Calendar

- ❑ **Simplicity** – Regardless of the way-cool features an application or device has, the bottom line is that it must be simple enough to use so that you won't be tempted to skip noting an appointment when you are rushed. If you can add a new date to your calendar in three or four steps, you're in good shape.

- ❑ **Accessibility** – While desktop computer applications are perfectly fine for when you're sitting in front of your computer, they aren't much help when you are not sitting in front of your computer, like when you are making your next appointment at the dentist and you have no idea if you are free on a given date. So make sure your calendar is automatically syncing to any other calendars you have.

- ❑ **The 'will you use it' factor** – Again, regardless of how cool a new Blackberry or iPhone is, if you don't use the calendar on it, it is an expensive paperweight that doubles as a phone. Really think about how you will use a device before you convince yourself that you can't live without it.

For most of my clients, I recommend a system where you can access the calendar wherever you are, which means one of two things:

1. You use a cell phone which you take everywhere.

2. You set up a system with software and hardware that allows you to access your calendar on multiple devices – your PC, a tablet, a cell phone, the web, etc.

Let's take a look at some options:

System	Simplicity	Accessibility
Office365/Outlook	Easy	Desktop, web, mobile devices
Google Calendar	Easy	Web, mobile devices
iCal	Easy on Apple devices	Can by synced to non-Apple devices, but may be difficult

There is no 'best one' for everyone. The idea is to find one that fits with your life, and then to use it consistently! If you do, you'll find that your life runs a great deal more smoothly than without a calendar.

What Goes in a Calendar?

Here is a list of things that should go in your calendar. You'll soon have time to add items to your calendar. Use this list to get you started.

Appointments	School/Work
Doctor, dentist, counselor, interviews	Due dates for projects
Birthdays and Anniversaries	Milestones for projects
Financial Reminders	Reminders to set up appointments
Pay rent, utilities, credit cards, etc.	**Fun**
Pay income and property taxes	Dinners/lunches with friends
Health Reminders	Vacations
Refill prescriptions	Club meetings
Set up annual check-up	**Car**
Set up bi-annual hygiene appt	Oil change reminders
All Meetings	Tune up reminders
Haircut/Clothing Reminders	New tire/rotation reminders

EXERCISE 2 — CALENDAR QUIZ

1. Why is using a calendar typically a good idea?

2. What are important considerations when choosing a calendar?

3. List three ways that using a calendar could make your life a bit easier.

   ❑ _____

   ❑ _____

   ❑ _____

Calendar Pro-Tips

Many people in business live and die by calendars, so here are a few additional tips to try when your life gets so chaotic that just having things on your calendar may not be enough. Have a look at the calendar below.

Besides being very busy, you should note that different items on the calendar use different colors (represented here in differing shades of gray). This labeling system is extremely useful when you have many different types of activities. On this calendar, we have intakes, phone calls, business meetings, client meetings, appointments for my children, and personal events.

Using colors in this way helps a great deal to quickly identify what needs to be done in a given day or week. A quick glance shows that I have to get my daughter to an appointment. If everything was the same color, I would have to read the text in each item to notice that.

Students can use this system, too. Use a different color for each subject you are taking, and then label quizzes, exams, projects and papers due in that class using the class color. That way, at a glance you can see that you have a midterm in Chem and a paper due in Lit without reading all of the text.

Breaking down Large Tasks

One issue I repeatedly see with clients is an inability to break things down into small chunks, leaving them to feel overwhelmed when a big assignment, or task, or event creeps up on them.

Breaking down tasks isn't that hard once you practice a bit. Let's look at these examples.

Breaking down a Paper Assignment

Let's say you have four weeks to do the paper, and the paper is due on October 31, and today is October 12. It's a ten-page research paper, and you need an annotated bibliography with five sources.

So, we have some information:

- ❑ We have just over two weeks to complete the report.
- ❑ On a good day, it takes us an hour to write one page, so we'll need 10 hours to write.
- ❑ We need to set aside time to go the library and do some research. That should take about three hours in total.
- ❑ We'll need extra time to edit and complete the bibliography, maybe four hours.

We now know that we need seventeen hours to do a really good job on this paper. And we know that going to the library should happen at the beginning, and that editing and finishing the biblio will likely be an end task just before turning the paper in.

This should give you enough information to break down the tasks and put them on the calendar as actual events:

- ❑ Go to the library
- ❑ Writing (several small chunks, likely)
- ❑ Edit and complete (one or two chunks)

Breaking down a Big Trip

You can use similar strategies to do any project or to prepare for any event.
Let's try a trip to Jamaica!

- ❑ You need to pick a time to go and make sure you can take the time off.
- ❑ You need to purchase airline tickets
- ❑ You need to arrange for a hotel or other accommodations.
- ❑ You need to arrange for ground transportation to and from the airport.
- ❑ You might want to make sure that you will have cell service while there.
- ❑ You may want to make sure that you have enough cash, and you may want to alert your credit card company that you will be out of the country.
- ❑ You may need to arrange for a pet or house-sitter, or someone to water your plants.

All of this is really more of a checklist, rather than a series of events, but that's okay. You can use your calendar to store tasks and to set aside time to work on them. As long as everything gets done, you're golden!

EXERCISE 3 — BREAKDOWN EXERCISE

Take a project you have been meaning to do, and break it down into chunks or steps:

Project name:_____

1. _____

2. _____

3. _____

4. _____

5. _____

6. _____

7. _____

8. _____

Using Alarms/Reminders

Using reminders is essential to remind you of upcoming events, so set reminders. Do remember a few things:

- ❑ For appointments that require travel, set the alarm at the time you need to leave, not the time you need to be there! Always 'book' the travel time on your calendar so that you have time to get to and from your appointment.

- ❑ You may also want to set two alarms for this type of appointment, in case you need to arrange a ride with someone. Set a reminder for this type of event the day before (to arrange the ride or to have the car) and at the time you need to leave.

- ❑ For events that don't have to be done at a certain time, but that you've put on your calendar to make sure you actually do the task, don't delete the reminder when it goes off. Delete the reminder when you have finished the task!

EXERCISE 4 — CALENDAR PRO-TIP QUIZ

1. What pro-tips can you use to improve your organization?

2. How can you use reminders and alarms more effectively?

3. How can you use calendars effectively for appointments that require travel?

EXERCISE 5 — USING YOUR CELL PHONE'S CALENDAR

We're going to take some time now to get organized with calendars.

1. Take out your phone, and navigate to the calendar app. Take a look at it and see if it is a proprietary application that will be hard to sync with your computer, or if it's one that does this automatically.

2. Go ahead and start putting in a few events.

3. Note that on your phone, you probably won't be able to set different colors for your events, the way you can on your computer. That's okay. You can go in later and set these on your computer.

4. When you get home today, ask your parents or roommates for their birthdays, and put those in as annually-repeating events on your calendar!

Filing Systems

Even though so much of our lives are digital now, you will still need to maintain some sort of paper-based filing system. It does not have to be anything elaborate. In fact, the simpler the better – if it's simple to use, you actually will use it!

To get started, I recommend an accordion-type file system. This is all you will need for a while, and later when you have more paperwork to store and save, you can move to a filing cabinet. You can buy accordian folders at any office supply store or online.

If you are paying your bills online, you probably don't need to keep paper bills or invoices unless you are using these bills for tax purposes (in which case, save them in a section called Taxes).

EXERCISE 6 — SET UP A FILING SYSTEM

We're going to hand out accordian folders to each student, and help you set up a filing system to use. To set up your filing system, take these steps:

1. Carefully write the following on each label:

- **Receipts/Taxes – Put your receipts from charitable contributions, prescription co-pays, items you have purchased for work, or any other items that might be tax deductible.**

- **Housing – Keep any rental agreements you have in this section.**

- **Health Records – Keep a copy of your birth certificate, your immunization records, and your insurance card in this section.**

- **Auto Insurance – Keep a copy of your auto insurance here.**

- **Renters Insurance – Keep a copy of your renters insurance here if you have it.**

- **School Records – Keep a copy of your diplomas and your most recent transcripts in this section.**

- **Employment Records – Keep a copy of any offer letters, information on unions, etc in this section.**

- **Personal Papers – Keep a copy of your social security card, your driver's license, and your passport here.**

- □ **Warranty Cards – Keep the original warranty cards you get with any big purchases, such as new phones.**

- □ **Miscellaneous – Keep other materials that don't have a 'home,' but need to be kept, in this section.**

2. Use this system *religiously*, and it will save you hours of looking for important documents.

3. What other important papers should you store in this folder? Can you think of other ways to use this type of filing system?

First Things First

The well-known time management guru Stephen Covey coined the term 'First Things First' a few decades ago, and it is just as relevant now as it was then. We spend too much time caught up in things that are not important but appear urgent, and too little time on things that are not (yet) urgent, but are very important. Have a look at the chart below.

		Importance
	sloth	School Projects Chores school home work F meetings of counselors
	Time-Wasters	Normal Work
	Interruptions	Crises
Urgency →	Deviantart Notifications Listening to Youtube. Writing somethingelse Other people	Deadlines Tests Studies

Take a careful look at this box – the axes indicate importance ('bad things will happen if I don't do this' or 'good things will happen if I do this') and the urgency with which we need to respond to something. Here's a description of these four areas:

❑ **Normal Work** – This is where most of your day should be spent, whether it's school work, or doing a job, or running a household. You know what you're supposed to be doing and you're doing it. Normal work should include planning – looking ahead and planning your day, week, month, and so on. This work is important, but not urgent if we stay on top of it.

❑ **Crises** – Dealing with a crisis is often annoying, and disrupts our ability to get our day-to-day 'job' done. Some crises just happen to us, but some crises are of our own making: forgetting an important assignment, not paying attention to a looming deadline, and so forth. Crises are both important and urgent; things must be done NOW.

❑ **Interruptions** – Interruptions 'feel' urgent, because they are vying for your attention. These include email, Facebook, text message notifications, phone calls, and so forth. Chimes, beeps, rings all are vying for our attention when we are trying to do our normal work. These are urgent in that they are happening in the here and now, but they frequently are not important. Spend some time going through your notification settings on your cell phone and computer to 'shut out' all but the most important notifications.

❑ **Time-Wasters** – We all have these, and sometimes, they are fine for us to indulge in – typically after work. These include gaming, watching YouTube videos, and social media. But, you can also waste time by cleaning your desk off for the fourth time this week instead of doing your work. You can go down a rat-hole doing far more research than you need to avoid doing the hard work of writing. Watch your time-wasters!

EXERCISE 7 — MAP OUT YOUR 'FIRST THINGS FIRST'

Next you're going to spend a little time mapping out how you typically spend your time in a given week:

1. **What activities belong in the Normal Work section? Don't forget to include both school/work and home activities like chores and errands.**

   ❑

   ❑

   ❑

   ❑

   ❑

   ❑

2. **What activities tend to fall into Crises? Think back to the last few weeks. What things 'blew up' and how could you have avoided that?**

   ❑

   ❑

   ❑

   ❑

3. Interruptions! What things interrupt you on a daily basis? Don't forget about all of the chimes and notifications you have set. You may also want to put down family members, if they interrupt your work.

   □

   □

   □

   □

4. Finally, our Time Wasters. For now, write down only the things that you turn to to avoid doing your work. You know what they are!

   □

   □

   □

   □

Now copy these items to the chart and then take a picture with your phone of that chart!

For the next few weeks, take a few minutes each evening to reflect on how you are spending your time. Refer back to this chart – are you doing things that will help you grow and develop new skills? Are you spending time with people you love and care for? Are you spending an adequate amount of time preparing for important things? Think about where your time goes, so that you can use it more wisely.

SECTION 3

BEING WELL

Your Physical and Mental Health

Once you have moved out on your own, one of the most important things you will be responsible for is your own health. This is especially important if you have been receiving ongoing care for any physical or mental health challenges. You are now responsible for understanding what medications you take and why you take them, and for setting up and attending all health appointments. You are also responsible for knowing when to get additional help, either for medical or psychological treatment.

You should have your own physician and your own dentist, and you should see them regularly. If you don't have a doctor or dentist, or if you don't *like* your doctor or dentist, it is up to you to find one you like and trust. Always remember that you must advocate for yourself! If you don't trust a doctor, or if you don't think they spend enough time with you, or if you don't think they understand your concerns, find another doctor.

Also remember that NO ONE has the right to mistreat you, embarrass you, or cause you any distress. Doctors sometimes tell us things we don't want to hear – that's fine, that is their job. But, they must treat you with respect and consult with you – not *tell* you – about how best to address your needs.

You can use the information below to help you locate a good doctor, dentist, or therapist.

Finding a Doctor

Decide what you're looking for in a doctor. For example, someone who is young and has innovative ideas, someone who is the same gender as you, someone who is associated with a particular hospital, etc.

You can ask friends or relatives if they have a doctor that they would recommend, you can check online using sites such as HealthGrades.com, and you should definitely check with your health insurance provider to see who is covered by your policy.

For any doctors you're considering using:

- ❑ Check the doctor's credentials with the state medical board
- ❑ Ensure that the doctor has a working knowledge about your conditions, both physical and psychological. **It is important to tell your doctor about your diagnosis, and about the medications that you take!**

Ensure:

- ❑ You'll have adequate access to the doctor and the staff, in person and by phone
- ❑ The doctor's office runs smoothly
- ❑ The doctor encourages two-way communication style and doesn't boss you around or hurry to get you out of his/her office
- ❑ You and the doctor have mutual respect which leads to trust

Going to the Doctor

Before:

- ❑ Be prepared! Write down items to discuss with the doctor, e.g.:
  - ▫ Ailments and symptoms you've experienced recently
  - ▫ Questions to ask, and concerns to mention to, your doctor
  - ▫ Your treatment to date and any medications you are taking
- ❑ Be prepared to give a urine sample (don't pee right before going to the doctor's office, do drink lots of fluids)

Bring:

- ❑ Health insurance card and/or insurance information
- ❑ List of all medications you're taking and/or the actual medications
- ❑ Medical/health records
- ❑ Check, credit card or cash to pay bill

During visit:

- ❑ Ask lots of questions and take notes, e.g.:
  - ▫ Tests that were administered
  - ▫ Results of tests and what they mean
  - ▫ Treatment options
  - ▫ Clarification of doctor's comments, advice and recommended treatment

If the doctor recommends/prescribes a course of action you're unsure of:

- ❑ Talk to a friend or family member you trust and ask his/her opinion
- ❑ Get a second (and perhaps third) opinion from another doctor

Always:

- ❑ Schedule a health check-up at least yearly
- ❑ Call your doctor if you have a fever higher than 103°
- ❑ Call your doctor if you have any unusual/unexplained pain anywhere in your body
- ❑ Call your doctor if you have any wounds that do not heal or are red, swollen, or tender for longer than a few days or if they get worse
- ❑ Call your doctor if you have lost or gained weight unexpectedly

EXERCISE 1 — HEALTH PROFESSIONAL QUIZ

1. **List three things that are important to know about your doctor.**

   ❏ _____
   ❏ _____
   ❏ _____

2. **When should you call the doctor?**

   ❏ _____
   ❏ _____
   ❏ _____

3. **What should you do if the doctor tells you something you don't understand or don't agree with?**

   ❏ _____
   ❏ _____
   ❏ _____

Medications

Approximately 4 of every 1000 prescriptions filled are incorrect (e.g., wrong dose, allergic reactions, wrong medication). It is up to you to make sure that your medications are correct and up to date.

❏ When a doctor prescribes you medication, always ask what that medication is any side effects.

❏ Always read the prescription label when you pick up your medications to make sure it is the medication prescribed.

❏ If you have more than one doctor prescribing you medication, make sure that you always update each doctor as to what medication you are currently taking.

❏ Always finish all medication unless otherwise instructed by your doctor.

❏ If you take medicine for depression or anxiety, **do not** stop taking the medication without first speaking to your doctor.

❏ Try to use one pharmacy for all of your prescriptions so that the pharmacist can alert you to potentially dangerous drug interactions and/or inappropriate prescriptions.

❏ If you notice that your medication does not seem to be working as it should, or if you have any unexpected side effects, contact your doctor as soon as possible.

EXERCISE 2 — MEDICATION QUIZ

1. **List three things that are important to know about medications your doctor prescribes.**

   ❑ _____

   ❑ _____

   ❑ _____

2. **When should you stop taking medication?**

   ❑ _____

   ❑ _____

   ❑ _____

3. **What should you always do when you pick up your medication from the pharmacy?**

   ❑ _____

   ❑ _____

   ❑ _____

Health Insurance

We talk elsewhere in this training about health insurance, but it's important to talk about it again. Right now (2018) it is unclear what the impact of rolling back ACA's health care policy will be in terms of cost and availability.

Here are some things to remember regardless of the status of policy that will likely remain unchanged:

❑ Having health insurance is vital for everyone, but especially for those who have special physical or emotional needs. Unfortunately, health insurance can be both expensive and difficult to obtain. To the extent that you can obtain and keep health insurance, do so – even if money is tight, resist the temptation to let your insurance lapse.

❑ Typically, the best way to get health insurance is through an employer if it is offered. Group insurance rates are generally less than individual policies, and depending on how long you are employed at that company, you are entitled to ongoing health benefits for up to 36 months after you leave the company through COBRA and Cal-COBRA programs.

❑ If you are enrolled in classes at a college or university, you may be eligible for health insurance through the campus office. Check with the student services office. Additionally, most colleges have free or low-cost clinics for routine health care.

❑ As it stands today, you cannot be denied health insurance if you have a pre-existing medical or psychiatric condition. However, that may change. If it does, you will need to continue your health insurance without fail, or potentially be denied health insurance on the open market. If you let your policy lapse more than 60 days, you may be denied medical insurance.

❑ If you need to obtain individual insurance, be prepared to disclose all past and current medical and psychological conditions. Health insurance companies usually check to see if the information you provide is complete, and will frequently disqualify people who have what is called a pre-existing condition. **If you are disqualified, you may qualify for insurance under one or more of these programs:**

  ▫ **Major Risk Policies through the State.** These programs predate ACA and may be offered again for those individuals with pre-existing conditions who may not be eligible for coverage in another way.

  ▫ **Medicare or Medi-Cal programs.** If you are receiving Social Security Disability Insurance or are low-income, you may be able to qualify for either (or both) of these low-cost insurance programs.

1. **Why is having health insurance important?**

2. **List three ways you might be able to get health care:**

   ❑ _____

   ❑ _____

   ❑ _____

First Aid & Emergency Preparedness

Okay, let's change gears and do what we can to keep from needing to use health insurance! Here is the list of the 10 most important items to have in your first aid kit, according to the American Red Cross. You should have these items in your home and your workplace at all times:

❑ Tweezers.

❑ Antiseptic wipes.

❑ First aid instructions.

❑ Triple antibiotic ointment.

❑ Adhesive bandages in a variety of sizes.

❑ Thermometer (the digital variety is safest).

❑ Sterile gauze pads in various sizes and cloth adhesive tape to secure them.

❑ Latex-free disposable gloves, to protect you from bodily fluids or other matter. Latex-free material prevents potential allergic reactions.

❑ Topical antihistamines and aspirin (or some other type of over-the-counter pain reliever recommended by your doctor).

❑ Your medications. If it is not feasible to keep extra medications in your first aid kit, then you and your family should know where your medications are at all times.

❑ It's also a good idea to take a certified Red Cross or American Heart Association CPR class. These are typically free or very low cost, and often available at community colleges. Make sure to take a class that covers both traditional CPR and also trains on how to use the new AEDs which are becoming increasingly common in public spaces.

You can also buy first aid kits through the American Red Cross website, *redcrossstore.org*. Your first-aid kit should include a sheet listing your family's known medical conditions, emergency contact numbers, and insurance information for hospitals and emergency medical services.

First Aid Procedures

The sooner you treat minor mishaps, the less likely they are to become major ones. To help you take the right action right away, use the chart of first aid procedures on the next page, along with instructions for what to do, what not to do, and when to call in the professionals.

1. Remember that the first thing to ALWAYS do in an emergency is to STAY CALM. Becoming panicky does nothing but waste energy and valuable time. Take a few deep breaths, think about what your options are, and then act.

2. The second thing you should do is to call out for help – one person can call 911 while the other person renders aid.

3. And remember, you should update your CPR training every two or three years so that you will remember what to do in case of an emergency.

	DO	DON'T	Call 911
Choking	DO – Call 911. *For a victim age one or older:* Have the person lean forward and, using the palm of your hand, strike his back between the shoulder blades five times. If that doesn't work, stand behind the victim, place one fist above the belly button, cup the fist with your other hand, and push in and up toward the ribs five times, as in the Heimlich. *If you're alone:* Press your abdomen against something firm, like a kitchen counter, or use your hands.	DON'T – Give water or anything else to someone who is coughing.	
Poisoning	DO – If a person is unconscious or having trouble breathing, call 911. In other cases, call the Poison Control Centers' national hotline (800-222-1222). Be prepared to tell what substance was involved, how much was taken and when, and the age and the weight of the victim.	DON'T – Wait until symptoms appear to call for help. Do not induce vomiting.	Seek medical attention
Open Wound	DO – Place a piece of sterile gauze (or a clean cloth) on the injury and apply direct pressure to stop the bleeding. For minor cuts and scrapes, wash with soap and water; follow with a thin layer of Vaseline or an antibiotic ointment and cover with a bandage.	DON'T – Wash or apply ointment to a wound that's large, deep, or profusely bleeding. Seek medical help. Don't remove protruding objects.	Call your doctor if the wound is a deep puncture; becomes infected; is accompanied by a fever; or has redness, swelling, or red streaks around it.
Bloody Nose	DO – Lean slightly forward and pinch your nose just below the bridge, where the cartilage and the bone come together. Maintain the pressure for 5 to 15 minutes. Pressing an ice pack against the bridge can also help.	DON'T – Tilt your head back.	Call your doctor if you can't stop the bleeding after 20 minutes or if it accompanies a headache, dizziness, ringing in the ears, or vision problems.
Object in Eye	DO – Try to dislodge a small particle by blinking several times. If it's not budging, rinse the eye by holding the lid open under a running tap (if possible, remove contact lenses first).	DON'T – Never rub your eyes. Even a tiny piece of dirt can scratch the cornea. Never try to remove an object that's deeply embedded.	Call your doctor if you cannot remove the object, or if pain persists
Sprain	DO – Alternately apply and remove ice every 20 minutes throughout the first day. Wrapping the joint with an elastic compression bandage and elevating the limb may also help. Stay off the injury for at least 24 hours. After that, apply heat to promote blood flow to the area.	DON'T – Work through the pain, or you risk doing more serious damage, like tearing the ligament.	If the injury doesn't improve in a few days, you may have a fracture or a muscle or ligament tear; call a doctor.
Burns	DO – Place the burn under cool running water, submerge it in a bath, or apply wet towels. Loosely bandage a first- or second-degree burn for protection.	DON'T – Put ice, butter or antibiotic cream on burns or pop blisters.	Call 911 for third-degree, electrical, and chemical burns. Go to the ER for a second-degree burn that's larger than your palm.
Head Injuries	DO – If the person is unconscious, call 911. If the struck area is bleeding, treat it as you would any other cut, but follow up with your doctor, as there may be internal injuries. Icing a small bump can help reduce the swelling.	DON'T – Leave the victim alone, especially when he's sleeping. Wake him up every three hours.	Call 911 if the victim exhibits seizures, dizziness, vomiting, nausea, or changes in behavior.

EXERCISE 4 — FIRST AID QUIZ

1. List five things that should be in your first aid kit:

   ❑ _____

   ❑ _____

   ❑ _____

   ❑ _____

   ❑ _____

2. What is the very first thing you should do in an emergency?

3. What is the second thing you should do in an emergency?

4. List one thing to do in each situation (see following page):

   ▫ **Choking:**

   ▫ **Poisoning:**

   ▫ **Open wound:**

   ▫ **Bloody nose:**

   ▫ **Object in eye:**

   ▫ **Sprain:**

   ▫ **Burns:**

   ▫ **Head injuries:**

Emergency Preparedness

Being prepared for an emergency is easier than you may think – but preparation is essential for everyone, especially for those of us who live in earthquake country. Take the time now to go through this section and make sure that you are prepared for an emergency.

Home Walkthrough

Every home has potential dangers. Once every six months, walk through your home and look for – and correct – the following situations:

1. **Unsecured furniture/fixtures** – Check to ensure that all heavy furniture is bracketed to the wall through one or more studs. Make sure that heavy mirrors and pictures are mounted using special weight-rated hooks. Make sure there is NOTHING heavy hanging or placed over or near beds!

2. **Breakable or heavy objects higher than waist level** – Make sure that all heavy objects are stored no higher than waist-high. For light-weight breakable objects, make sure that they are affixed to the shelf with museum clay to keep them from moving and falling during an earthquake.

3. **Hanging plants** – Make sure all hanging plants are adequately mounted through the ceiling, preferably into a stud, and make sure that if they swing during an earthquake they will not swing through a window or into a mirror.

4. **Flammable materials near heat sources** – Never store anything flammable near a water heater, furnace, stove, oven, or radiator.

EXERCISE 5 — HOME WALKTHROUGH EXERCISE

When you get home tonight, go through your home or apartment and make a list below of the things you might want to change. List them here:

- ❑ _____
- ❑ _____
- ❑ _____
- ❑ _____
- ❑ _____
- ❑ _____

Home Supplies

During a major disaster, you may not be able to get help for up to seven days. Roads may be blocked, utility services out, and stores may be out of food and water. The best plan is to make sure that you always have enough supplies for you and your family – including pets – to last for at least three and preferably seven days.

- ❑ **Water** – Each person needs 3 gallons of water per day for drinking, washing, and cooking.

- ❑ **Food** – Make sure that you have non-perishable foods to feed everyone in your family for at least three days. Include high fat, high energy food sources such as peanut butter, dried meats, granola bars, aseptic milk packages, and juice boxes.

- ❑ **Heat** – Remember that the power and gas may go out during an emergency. Keep a supply of firewood on hand, but make sure to visually inspect the chimney for damage before lighting a fire. If you have any doubts, don't light the fire.

- ❑ **Cooking Heat** – Barbeques make a great emergency stove, but remember to NEVER use charcoal inside or in an enclosed area. If you camp, consider using your camp stove, preferably outside.

- ❑ **Medication** – A good reason to always keep your prescriptions filled is so that you will be prepared in case of an emergency. Try to always refill when you have less than one week's supply.

EXERCISE 6 — BASIC SUPPLIES AND SAFETY QUIZ

1. **How much fresh water should you have on hand for each person, for each day?**

2. **What should you never use inside a home for cooking or heating?**

3. **How many days should you plan on having food for? What sort of food do you think you should have on hand?**

Car Supplies

Remember that there's a good chance that an emergency may happen while you are away from home – and, that it may be very difficult to get home quickly. Always keep the following items in your car:

❑ **Cell phone and charger** – Cell phones are great in an emergency, but absolutely useless if the battery is dead. Always keep a charger with an adapter in your car. You may also want to purchase a solar charger for your phone.

❑ **Flashlight** – An obvious choice are the new crank-battery models.

❑ **Food and water** – Always keep a few bottles of water and some power bars or other high-energy, high-fat snacks in your car.

❑ **Sturdy walking shoes** – If you need to walk any distance, you will need to have good shoes. If you don't always wear comfortable shoes, keep a pair in the car.

❑ **Cash (a few bucks)** – Coins and a few bills are useful.

❑ **Blanket or warm jacket** – In case you are caught in inclement weather, make sure you have something to keep you warm until you can reach help.

EXERCISE 7 — CAR SUPPLIES QUIZ

1. **List three things you should keep in your car.**

   ❑ _____

   ❑ _____

   ❑ _____

2. **Why is it a good idea to keep a cell phone charger in your car? How will that help during an emergency?**

3. **Why would you keep a blanket and shoes in your car?**

Emergency Kits

Ideally, you should have two emergency kits – one for home and one for your car. Kits should include the following items:

❑ Food and water for 3 days	❑ First aid kit
❑ Radio and batteries	❑ Blankets
❑ Flashlight and batteries	❑ Medications
❑ Cell phone and charger	❑ Walking shoes
❑ Toiletries	❑ Copies of personal papers
❑ Large plastic bags	❑ $100 in small bills

EXERCISE 8 — EMERGENCY SUPPLIES EXERCISE

1. What other items do you think would be important to have in your emergency kit? Look at the graphic above for ideas, and add them to the list on the left.

2. What 'creature comfort' items might you want to keep in your kit to keep you entertained, to help you feel calm, or to de-stress?

3. What one thing would be hard to do without? How could you accommodate that?

EXERCISE 9 — DISASTER PLAN EXERCISE

When you get home, fill out the form below with your family or roommates. Make copies for each person in your household, keep one in your wallet and one in your emergency kit. If you don't have a kit, work with your family or to create one that will be easily accessible in case of an emergency!

Contact Information			Emergency Location Information
1.	Ph.	Cell	Gas shut off:
2.	Ph.	Cell	
3.	Ph.	Cell	Water shut off:
4.	Ph.	Cell	
Out of Area Contact		Cell	Electrical panel:
Mailing Address		Email	
Meeting Locations			Emergency kit:
In House:			
In Neighborhood:			American Red Cross: 1 202 303-4498
In Town:			FEMA: 1 800 621-3362
Out of Town:			Weather Service: 1 202 482-6090

The Law and First Responders

I'll start this section by saying that I hope you never have any cause to use the information in this section, but we're going to read it just in case. Because, stuff happens.

First off, remember that all law enforcement and first responder personnel (police, firefighters, paramedics, etc.) have a very important job to do, and when they are doing their job, they are all business. They have very little patience for anything other than what they are trying to do – dealing with a crisis or a potential crisis.

To that end, ALWAYS comply with what an officer or first responder tells you to do. **DO NOT ARGUE**. It does no good, and will only make them mad and get you into (more) trouble. If you are told to pull over on the freeway, do so as soon as it is safe. If a firefighter tells you to get out of your home, do so. If a paramedic tells you that you are injured and should go to the hospital, go to the hospital.

Take several deep breaths and calm yourself down. Answer all questions honestly and calmly. If you feel like you are being overwhelmed and are becoming overly anxious to the point where you feel like 'breaking', explain to the officer (or whomever) that you have a condition that causes you to panic more easily than other people, and that you need to go somewhere quiet. If you stay calm, and quietly explain that you are about to 'break', the officer should comply.

Do know that not all law enforcement and first responders are aware of how autism or mood disorders or ADHD impact people, let alone how it impacts you. **Therefore, as stressful as it is, you must be the one to supply the information in such a way so that the officer does not see you as belligerent or problematic, but as a person with a real need, such as a quiet place to talk.** Read this next paragraph, and try to memorize it, using your own words. If you do so, you will be more likely to calmly give this information to someone when needed.

I have [name your diagnosis]. This condition makes it very difficult for me to handle stressful situations. Please be patient with me, and if possible, please take me to a quiet location before asking me questions. Thank you.

EXERCISE 10 — DEALING WITH FIRST RESPONDER QUIZ

1. **What should you never do with any first responder?**

2. **What might happen if you start screaming or running away from a police officer?**

3. **What can you do to try to calm yourself down in a situation like this?**

Drugs and Alcohol

Like with the previous section, let's hope that you never have to refer to this information again. But we are going to talk about drugs and alcohol, because they can have a profound effect on your life beyond just getting high.

Alcohol is a depressant. Because many of our clients have depression or a tendency toward depression, I strongly urge them to not drink, or to drink very rarely and only in moderation. The reason for this is very simple — if you are depressed to begin with and you take a depressant, you get more depressed. If you are taking an antidepressant and drink alcohol, it has the same effect as not taking your antidepressant. Which is pretty silly.

If you find yourself wanting to drink, ask yourself why. Many people who drink regularly do so because they feel the need to 'self-medicate' with alcohol. If this is the case, that you want to drink to feel better, then your best course of action is to speak with your psychiatrist or health care worker — it could mean that your medications are not working properly, or that you need therapy, or some other life change to not need to self-medicate.

The same goes for using drugs. Some of my clients smoke weed, for example. Marijuana has more or less the same effect as drinking alcohol — most strains act as a depressant. Again, if you find yourself wanting to smoke dope on a regular basis, you need to ask yourself why — and treat the real problem without self-medicating.

A few other things about drugs and alcohol: not only do they counteract commonly used prescriptions, but they can be downright deadly with a few of them.

If, for example, you are on anti-anxiety medication, mood stabilizers, **or any psychotropic drug whatsoever** (which covers pretty much every drug prescribed for neurodiverse symptoms), drinking alcohol while on these medications can depress your nervous system to such an extent that you pass out and literally stop breathing and die. Big fun.

If you are on stimulants for attention deficit, note that taking any stimulants whatsoever – even drinking coffee – can cause heart palpitations and extreme edginess. Taking a prescription stimulant with a recreational stimulant such as methamphetamine (commonly meth or crank) or cocaine, can indeed kill you.

As for all of the other recreational drugs, just don't do them. It's not a moral issue, but one of life and death for those folks who are on prescription medication. Find a better way to feel better.

EXERCISE 11 — DRINKING AND DRUGGING QUIZ

1. **Why does it make no sense to drink if you have depression or are taking an anti-depressant?**

2. **What are the potential side-effects of drinking on medication?**

3. **What are the potential side-effects of taking street stimulants if you take ADHD medication?**

Safety

This section is devoted to safety and self-defense and is in no way promoting the use of violence to solve conflicts. That being said, should you be attacked it is important for you to be able to yourself. Perhaps the most important part of self-defense, however, is adopting safe practices.

General Safety Practices

Before You Leave

- ❑ Plan before you go. Always tell a family member or friend where you are going and when you will return.
- ❑ Keep your cell phone on you and keep it charged.
- ❑ Carry ID with you at all times, and don't carry a lot of cash, or wear flashy jewelry.

On the Road

- ❑ Always be aware of your surroundings, whether in a car, on foot, or on a bike.
- ❑ Don't wear sound cancelling headphones when you are traveling. If you wear them you won't hear an approaching car or attacker. Listen to your surroundings.
- ❑ Avoid unpopulated areas, deserted streets, and overgrown trails. Especially avoid poorly lit areas at night.
- ❑ Trust your intuition about a person or an area. It you are unsure about an area, or feel unsafe, leave immediately.
- ❑ Ignore verbal harassment. Use discretion in acknowledging strangers. Look directly at others and be observant, but keep your distance and keep moving.
- ❑ Be careful if anyone in a car asks you for directions; if you answer, keep at least a full arm's length from the car.
- ❑ If you think you are being followed, change direction and head for open stores, theaters or a lighted house.
- ❑ Have your door key ready before you reach your home.
- ❑ Call police immediately if something happens to you or someone else, or you notice anyone out of the ordinary. See something, say something!

When You're at Home

- ❑ If you are home alone, keep doors and windows locked.

- ❑ Make sure your cell phone is nearby and charged.

- ❑ If someone knocks on the door and you are not expecting anyone, peek through a window to see who it is before answering. If you don't know them, see if they leave. If they don't, call the police.

- ❑ Keep curtains and window blinds drawn, but keep a few lights on. Most burglars will not want to break into a house with activity. Turn on the TV or music!

EXERCISE 12 — SAFETY QUIZ

1. **List five things that you can do immediately to keep yourself safer at home and in the community?**

   ❑ _____

   ❑ _____

   ❑ _____

   ❑ _____

   ❑ _____

2. **What should you do if you see something or someone suspicious?**

   Get out of their sight.

   Record.

3. **What two things should you always have on you when you leave home?**

Run, Hide...

1. If you find yourself in a dangerous situation where someone is directly threatening you but is unarmed, the best thing to do is yell FIRE! and either hide or run as fast as you can to where other people are.

2. If you find yourself in a dangerous situation where someone is directly threatening you and is armed, follow whatever instructions they give you. Stay calm, look down.

... and Defend

If you cannot run or hide, and feel you need to take action (particularly if there are others with you), follow these steps:

1. Commit to your actions. If you start this line of defense, you must follow through.

2. Improvise weapons: chairs, laptops, keys, whatever is at hand.

3. Act as a group and attack all at once.

4. Act as aggressively as possible: yell, shout, throw things to disorient the attacker.

5. Grab attacker's limbs and head, take them to the ground. Disarm the attacker, hold them face down by kneeling on his/her back or stepping on arms until help arrives.

Self-Defense

Learning self-defense basics may be a good idea, but do know that it takes time to practice to become proficient in these techniques. The best defense is nearly always begin safe to start with and then escaping as necessary.

EXERCISE 13 — RUN, HIDE, DEFEND PRACTICE

We'll take some time now to 'walk through' an active shooter situation.
Pick one person to be the 'bad person'.

1. Talk about how you might get out of the situation. Where are the doors, windows, etc.

2. What weapons are available? How might you use them?

3. Practice acting as a 'gang', yelling and screaming and threatening (verbally!) the attacker to disorient him/her.

SECTION 4

PERSONAL FINANCES

Overview

Finances are pretty simple when you are just starting out. You have money coming in (from parents, from your job) and money going out (for rent, utilities, food, fun, insurance, etc.).

The goal of this game is to have enough money coming in so that you can cover all of the money going out. This takes some short and long term planning, it takes some attention, and it takes a little bit of time, but once you get the hang of it, it will become much easier.

Starting a Budget

The first and most important task you need to do is to create a simple budget, which is really no more than a list of the money coming in, and an estimate of money going out. There isn't any great magic to this, other than to be realistic. Have a look:

Expense	Cost	Totals
Rent	$900	
Groceries	$400	
Fast Food	$200	
Cable/Internet	$75	
Electricity/Gas	$85	
Entertainment	$100	
Cell phone	$90	
	Income	$2200
	Expenses	$1850

That's not too hard, is it? All you need to do is to figure out, to the best of your ability, how much you spend each month, and what you are spending it on. Some things are reliable (*fixed costs*) like your rent or a car payment. These costs generally do not change from month to month.

So when you create your budget, start with the costs that are always the same month to month, for example, rent, prescription costs, auto loans. These are easy.

Your turn! Try your hand at creating a budget starting with *fixed costs.*

Expense	Cost	Totals
Rent		
Prescription co-pays		
Student loan		
Bus pass		
Gym membership		
Xbox subscription		
Other:		
Other:		
Other:		
Other:		
	Expenses	$

Non-Fixed Cost Items

Other costs, like most utilities, grocery and eating out costs, entertainment costs, and auto costs (gas and repairs) may be similar from month to month, but not exactly the same – and some months, they may be very high or very low. Next, you need to figure out the average cost per month for the items that are not always the same.

To do this, look at your bank statements and tally up how much you have spent on each item over a period of at least three months, and preferably six months.

Then, divide this number by how many months you used for your tally. This number is a good starting place for your budget. For example, if your cell phone bill was $56.17 in April, $32.99 in May, and $78.09 in June, you'd add these totals up ($167.25) and divide by three ($55.75). This number then is your average, which you can use for your budget. If you'd like, you can round the number up to give yourself a little wiggle room; for example, call this number $60/month.

You would do this exercise for all of your expenses, and you have the preliminary workings of a budget. There's a budget worksheet at the end of this chapter for you to fill in to get started.

EXERCISE 2 — ESTIMATING COSTS

In the table below, see if you can estimate some of your expenses. If need be, you can always make the data up. For example, how much money do you spend each week on gaming, going to events, paying college fees, going to boba tea or Starbucks?

Expense	Average Monthly Cost	Totals
	Expenses	$

1. Why do you think it's important to estimate these costs?

2. What challenges do you think estimating costs might bring, if you don't spend all of that allocated funding one month, but need two or three months' worth of funding the following month?

3. What other tools or strategies could you use to ensure you have money when you need it?

Paying Your Bills and Balancing Your Accounts

At least once a month, and maybe twice a month, you will need to pay your bills. Usually, your rent or mortgage is due on the first of each month, and you will likely have a handful of other bills due at about the same time. However, other bills will arrive later in the month, and if you wait until the beginning of the following month, they may be late. So, you'll need to pay your bills more than once a month to avoid damage to your credit and accruing late fees.

The easiest solution is to add a repeating event on your calendar for the beginning and middle of the month, to remind you to pay your bills. Remember the section on organizing and using a calendar? We also talked about how to file your incoming bills into your accordion style filing system. All you have to do is file the bills as they come in, and twice a month go through that month's partition and pay whatever is due. Simple!

There are essentially three ways to pay your bills:

1. **Write checks and mail them in** — This is the **low**-tech, tried and true way, but is a bit time consuming, and requires that you manually add the check number, amount, and payee (who you made the check out to) into your check register, a spreadsheet, or into a financial application such as Quicken.

2. **Pay bills electronically (manual)** — This method takes a bit more set-up, but overall is much easier to do. You can pay many of your bills directly to the company you owe (such as PG&E or AT&T) by logging into their website and then into your account, free of charge. A simpler way is to either use your bank's electronic bill pay service (such as Well Fargo's Bill Pay) or to use an application such as Quicken to pay your bills. Either of these services allow you to pay all of your bills with a few clicks of a mouse. An added advantage of an application like Quicken is that it will allow you to download all of your financial statements from various banks, and can be used to create and maintain budgets and manage your all of your assets in one place.

3. **Pay bills electronically (automatic)** — This is the same method as above, but instead of manually selecting which bills to pay and when (and how much to pay), you can set up the applications to pay your bills automatically on the same day of each month.

At the end of each month, you will need to go through all of your cashed checks or payments, all of your deposits and transfers, and ensure that what you believe you have in your checking account is the same as what the bank says you have. If not, you can ask a representative of your bank to help you track the difference.

Even if you use autopay for your bills, you should get into the habit of checking your finances at least once a week. This alerts you to any strange activity or fraud, keeps you apprised of your balance, and let's you ensure that payments you have made have indeed gone through (paying a bill doesn't 'count' until received!).

EXERCISE 3 — SET REMINDERS TO CHECK FINANCES AND PAY BILLS

1. **Grab your phone and set a repeating weekly reminder to check your bank account(s).**

2. **List three reasons below why it's important to do this!**

   ❏ _____

   ❏ _____

   ❏ _____

Using Mint.com

A great way to create and manage personal budgets and to stay on top of your finances is to use Mint.com. This is a free aggregator application available from Intuit, which you can find at: https://www.mint.com. In order to use this application, you will need your account numbers for your checking and credit card accounts, and your login information. This may sound scary, but Intuit is a well-known company, and hundreds of thousands of people trust them with this information, including EvoLIbri! They also make QuickBooks, Quicken, and TurboTax.

1. Grab your phone again, or a laptop, and access or download Mint.com.

2. Enter in your account information, and let Mint.com download all of your transactions.

3. Go through your transactions, and categorize them by type. Mint.com has categories such as Groceries, Movies, Rent, Clothes, and so forth. You can also create your own categories.

4. Over time, Mint will 'learn' how to categorize most of your expenses, but you should still check your transactions once in awhile to make sure they are going into the right 'buckets'.

5. Next, you use Mint.com's budget tool. Click Budgets on the top toolbar, and then click the plus sign Create a Budget button to start.

6. Add in all of the expenses you have identified in previous exercises, and set up notifications so that if you spend more in one given area, Mint will notify you with a text message!

Types of Financial Accounts

You probably already know the names of the different financial accounts, but we'll look at them again so that you have a good understanding of what each type is and what they are good for.

❑ **Checking Accounts** – A checking account is simply a place to keep your money so that you can have easy access to it at all times. Checking accounts generally do not earn interest on the money that is in them, and so are best used for your normal monthly income and expenses (money comes in, money goes out). You can access the funds in a checking account by writing a check, using a debit card, or using an ATM card to get cash from your account. Remember that you need to have enough money in your checking account to cover all of your transactions or you will pay for overdraft charges (the fee that the bank charges when you 'bounce' a check or transaction).

❑ **Savings Accounts** – Savings accounts earn interest and are a good place to 'park' small amounts of money temporarily. For example, if you are saving to buy a new TV, you may want to open a savings account and put in a little money each month until you have enough for the TV. Then, you can transfer the money from your savings account to your checking account and use it for your purchase. This way, the money is not in your checking account (where it can be easily spent) but not invested in a long-term investment instrument such as stocks or bonds so that you can access the funds when you need them. You can get savings accounts at your regular bank, or from a different organization.

❑ **Money Market Accounts** – Money market accounts are a hybrid investment instrument that is relatively new compared to savings accounts. These accounts generally require a minimum balance at all times (usually $500, sometimes more or less), but earn more interest than a standard savings account. Money market accounts usually have check cashing privileges and sometimes debit cards as well, and are good for larger amounts of money that you don't want invested in a long-term instrument, but they do carry some risk.

❑ **IRA or 401k Accounts** – These accounts are used for only one purpose – to save money for your retirement without incurring the taxes on this money until you use it. The money you can add to this account each year depends on your age and your income, so check with your employer or the person who does your taxes. Your employer may also allow you to automatically make a monthly contribution to a 401k program before income taxes are taken out, and may even contribute a certain amount of money to your retirement plan as well. Note that if you take money out of this account before you are 59.5 years of age, you will pay a hefty penalty, so this should always be considered a long-term investment. Roth IRAs are a little different in that they are not tax-deductible but are tax-deferred.

❑ **Stocks, Bonds and Treasury Bills** – These are also typically used for long-term investments, and are complicated enough that we won't go too deep into them. Briefly, these financial tools allow you to invest some of your money into a company, a certain type of material (commodity), or a government (city, county, state or federal) with the hope of earning income on your investment. If the company does well, the stock goes higher, and you earn money. If a city takes out a loan (a bond bill) and pays the money back, you earn income. However, if the company goes under, or the city does not pay it's loan back, you can lose money. Some of these investments have guaranteed earnings, most do not. We'll go into these a bit later.

❑ **The Mattress** – Yes, the mattress. Or a coffee can, or an envelope or some other container in which you can hide some cash away. Obviously, this is not a real financial instrument, but it's a good idea to have a small stash of cash in your home for emergencies (this does not include midnight pizza runs!). If we have an earthquake, flood or fire, or if you need to call a cab to get to the hospital, you'll be glad you have $100 or so on hand to get you through.

Student Checking Accounts

Many of you have or will have student checking accounts. These are accounts that are under the 'umbrella' of your parent's checking account, and are available for teens and young adults. This is an excellent way to start learning about banking, managing a budget, and saving money. All major banks make these available. Here are some tricks to know:

❑ Student accounts should be free. If the bank is charging you, then it isn't a student account. Talk to a banker.

❑ Make sure that you set 'overdraft protection' OFF on your account. This way, if you don't have money to buy that boba tea, you won't get your boba tea, but you will also not get charged $25 for not having enough money to cover the expense.

❑ You should get both an ATM card and checks with your account. Most teens and young adults don't use checks, so make sure you put them some place safe. Your ATM card should also be some place safe, preferably in your wallet, on your body, at all times. If you are not good about keeping your wallet with you, then leave it in a drawer or other location.

❑ Check your accounts regularly! It is important to keep an eye on your money!

The Anatomy of a Check

Below is a garden variety check. You will fill it out as follows:

❑ **Date:** This is today's date and year.	❑ _____**Dollars:** This is where you spell out the amount of the check.
❑ **Pay to the order:** This is the person you are paying.	❑ **Memo:** This is where you can make a note about the check.
❑ **$:** This is the amount, in numerical format, you are paying.	❑ **Signature Line:** The line on the bottom right is where you sign your name.

```
                                                              0000

                                      DATE_____20___

PAY TO THE
ORDER OF  _____  $ [        ]

_____ DOLLARS  🔒

MEMO  _____   _____
  ⑈0 ⑈ 2 3 4 5 6 7 8 9⑈:   0 ⑈ 2 3 4 5 6 7 8 9⑈⑈    ⑈ 2 3 4
```

Those wacky numbers at the bottom of every check? Those are your:

❑ **Bank routing number:** This is a unique number given to every financial institution. It identifies the bank and is always nine digits long. It is almost always the number on the left side of the check.

❑ **Account number:** This is a unique number given to every customer at a given bank. It identifies you. It can be of varying length and is typically to the right of the routing number.

❑ **Check number:** If present, this number should be the same number as printed on the upper right of the check, and identifies the specific check

These three numbers work together to ensure that the money is paid by the right bank (routing number), the right person (account number), and on the right check.

The Anatomy of a Credit Card or ATM

Below is a garden variety credit card – ATM or debit cards typically look the same.
They will have:

Front:

- ❏ Your bank name
- ❏ Your 16-digit account number
- ❏ The expiration date of this card
- ❏ Your name

Back:

- ❏ A place for your signature
- ❏ The CVC/security code

Also:

- ❏ ATM cards require a PIN to use. Don't write this on the card!

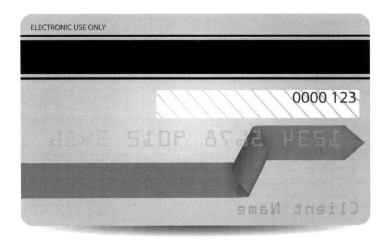

EXERCISE 5 — DIFFERENT TYPES OF FINANCIAL ACCOUNTS

List three different types of accounts that you think you might use in the next five years.

1.

2.

3.

Different Types of Credit and Loans

What happens when you don't have enough money to pay for what you need at this very moment, or want the convenience of a credit card? Now we look at different types of loans.

❏ **Credit Cards** – Credit cards are probably the most common type of loan – and frequently the one that gets most people into trouble. Credit cards are issued by banks, and are used to purchase items or services. At the end of the month, the bank will send you a detailed invoice, telling you how much you spent. The idea (for you) is to pay off the entire amount each month. The idea (for the bank) is for you to NOT pay off the entire amount, so that they can charge you interest on the balance you carry from month to month. Better yet, you forget to pay the bill on time, and then they can sock you with a late fee, and the interest, and maybe even raise your interest rate!

You get the point. Finance charges on credit cards range from about 11% to 27%. That's a lot of money to pay a bank for a loan. The key here is to never charge more than you can easily pay off in a few months. If you're not sure you can, look at another type of loan.

❏ **Unsecured Loans** – Unsecured loans are small loans that the bank will give you based on your good credit and your credit alone. This means that they tend to be difficult to get until you have substantial credit which is nearly flawless. Unsecured loans for most of us mere mortals tend to be for small amounts – $5000 or less – and generally are available for folks who don't really need loans. Go figure.

❏ **Secured Loans** – Secured loans are the most common bank loans, and the most common secured loan is a mortgage. Basically, a secured loan is where a bank or other lending institution, lends you money using your personal property as collateral. For example, let's say you buy a house for $500,000 and you have $100,000. You 'put down' the $100,000 to buy the house, and the bank lends you $400,000. You make payments to the bank every month to pay off the loan.

If you miss several payments, the bank can take your house and sell it, so that they can get their money back. Needless to say, when you enter into a loan like this, it is important to make sure that you can actually pay the monthly payments. If not, the bank has the right to take your property away, leaving you with nothing, you will have bad credit for a long time, and you won't be able to get another loan until your credit is okay again.

Importance of Good Credit and Protecting Your Identity

Much of your ability to buy a car or a home will depend on how good your credit is. It may not seem like a big deal to miss a payment once in a while, or to be late in paying a few bills, but over time, these few 'oops' moments can add up to a bad credit rating. You won't even know you have a bad credit rating until you apply for a loan, a new credit card – or worse yet – apply for a job that is contingent on a clean credit report (yep, that's right – some companies will not hire you if you don't have good credit).

Besides doing the obvious (paying your bills on time), you can and should check your credit rating from time to time. You should check your credit report once a year, and you may want to check it a few months before you intend to make a significant purchase, and will need to apply for a loan. Either way, it is simple to check your credit, and you can frequently do it for free. There are three main companies that keep financial data on people in the US: Experian, Equifax, and TransUnion. By law, each of these companies must share their data with you, free of charge, once a year. To do so, go to www.annualcreditreport.com and follow the directions to get your credit report. Note that many other companies claim to offer free reports as well, but they are usually selling services you may not want or need.

Besides knowing what your credit rating is, you should check your credit report to ensure that no one has been using your identity (and your good credit) for their own profit. Identity theft comes in many forms, but a common form is for someone to apply for a credit card under your name, but at a different mailing address – so that you never get the bills, and don't find out until it's too late. Then, the person charges hundreds or thousands of dollars on that credit card, and never pays the bills. Guess whose credit rating suffers? Yours! You can fix this problem by contacting the issuing credit card company and filing a report, but this can take many months to clear up. In the meantime, keep checking your report to make sure you're safe!

What Is a Credit Score?

Oy! All of these boring phrases. But this is important. It's kind of like playing a video game (that is your life) and you've acquired points that tell other players about your reliability. Your credit score shows other people your history and ability to pay your bills. That's it. If you have a great credit score, banks and the like will clamber to give you loans so that you can buy homes, start a business, buy a car, or get a bunch of cash so that you can pursue any number of your dreams.

How Do You Improve Your Credit Score?

You can change it by paying your bills on a regular basis, reducing the amount of money you have borrowed. That's how you can change it for the better. You can change it for the worse by NOT paying your bills, or by forgetting you HAVE bills to begin with.

What really stinks is that it takes a lot longer to show you are good with your bills than it does to show that you aren't good with them. If you forget a payment, it's not the end of the world, but these things add up and eventually your credit suffers. Once your credit has suffered it takes at least a couple of years paying your bills on time for your score to recover.

Who Checks Your Credit History?

Your credit history is subject to review in a lot of different areas. If you ever want a credit card, this is a good way to start developing credit, but it can also be a double edged sword in that you can easily ding your credit by missing a payment. Here's who checks:

- ❑ **Apartments and home rentals:** Most rentals or leases check your credit history. If you have a history of eviction or missed payments, this will knock against your chances at getting that dream apartment you've been waiting for. The number one way to get an eviction is by not paying your rent. Future landlords will not look favorably on evidence of this habit and will likely deny your application.

- ❑ **Car loans:** You want to buy a car but cannot afford the total upfront? You won't be able to buy a car with credit if your history is bad.

- ❑ **Phone companies and internet service providers**: Even mobile providers and other services check your credit history before approving you for service.

- ❑ **Even some jobs!!** Increasingly, employers are looking at credit history when hiring a new employee.

EXERCISE 6 — LOANS AND CREDIT QUIZ

1. What are common types of loans?

2. What is a common way that people get into trouble with their credit?

3. How is credit established?

4. Why is it important to check your credit?

5. How can you check your credit?

6. What 'bad things' can happen if you have bad credit?

Risk Management & Insurance

I remember when I fully understood the concept of insurance. Ironically, it was when I was sitting at a blackjack table in Lake Tahoe, and the dealer had an ace showing on the table. He asked if any of the players would like to purchase insurance, in case he had a 10 or face card underneath, in which case, he would have a blackjack, and we would lose, even if we had a blackjack as well.

This was risk management – by buying insurance, we were managing the risk of us possibly losing. All insurance is basically the same as the insurance at a blackjack table – you purchase insurance against the possibility of getting sick or needing to go to the hospital in an emergency (health insurance), or for the possibility that you die at a young age and can't take care of your children (life insurance), or for the possibility that you become seriously disabled and can no longer work to support yourself (long term care/disability insurance). Other types of insurance include auto insurance (mandatory if you drive a car) and renters insurance (optional if you rent), which cover your losses in case of theft or an accident.

Most large employers offer health insurance at either a discounted rate to their employees, or pay for part of the cost. If you are offered insurance at your place of work, it is usually wise to take it. If it is not offered, or if you are not working, it is generally still wise to purchase it. Most people taking this class will be receiving health insurance through their parents' plans until age 26. However, after this time, you will be responsible for your own insurance. And at the time of this writing, having health insurance is mandatory for everyone!

❑ **Health** – Health insurance is probably the most important insurance to have. Nearly everyone gets sick, or will need medication, or will need to go to the hospital at some point. Health insurance either pays for all of these costs, or part of them. Some people don't believe that health insurance is important for young people, because they don't get sick or as seriously sick, as older people. While that may or may not be true, healthcare costs are very, very high, and if you don't have insurance and end up in the hospital for something as relatively simple as to have your appendix removed, you may well end up owning $50,000 or more. Most people believe that it is far wiser to pay for health insurance month by month and maybe never need it than be faced with a huge bill such as this.

❑ **Life** – Life insurance is generally purchased to provide money to your dependents in the event of your early death, and how much insurance you buy is usually based on how much you estimate your children and spouse may need to live if you died today. Most young people don't carry life insurance until they are married and/or have children, though some people decide to buy a policy when they are young when the costs are lower to get a better rate for the rest of their lives.

❑ **Long-Term Care/Disability** – These types of insurance will provide money to you in the event that you have to stay in the hospital for a very long time, or if you become seriously disabled and cannot work anymore.

Important Notes about Healthcare

If you have a diagnosis such as Autism, ADHD, or Bipolar Disorder, you have what is known as a pre-existing condition. Under current federal law, you must not be denied coverage based on this, but that law is currently in jeopardy of being rescinded, which may make health insurance difficult and costly to obtain unless you are working for a company that offers it. Talk to an insurance broker about this if need be.

Another important thing to remember about healthcare is that aside from some specific exceptions, you can only enroll in new healthcare programs, or change healthcare programs, once a year, typically between November 1 and December 15. Again, talk to an insurance broker if you have any questions!

EXERCISE 7 — INSURANCE QUIZ

1. **Why can insurance be very important?**

2. **What types of insurance will you likely need?**

3. **What type of insurance is mandatory to have?**

4. **When can you enroll in a new healthcare plan?**

Taxes

You may have heard the saying that the only two things that are for certain in life are death and taxes, meaning that regardless of anything else, these two things are inevitable. No one likes paying taxes, but we like having clean water to drink that flows from our faucets, roads to travel on, firefighters we can call, schools we can attend, and a whole host of other goodies that we take for granted and that our taxes pay for. So, yes, they are inevitable in our modern world.

There are several different taxes you will probably pay throughout your lifetime:

- ❑ **Sales tax** – From the first purchase you made at GameStop or any other store, you paid sales tax (unless you live in one of the few states with no sales tax). This tax is added to most purchases and is collected by store and passed along to the State to help pay for local infrastructure and running the government.

- ❑ **Income (employment) tax** – Income tax is just like it sounds – tax that is based on how much money you earn. The theory is that the more you make, the more you pay, and for many of us, one third or more of our earned income goes to the state and federal governments.

- ❑ **Property tax** – If and when you buy a house or a condo, or any other type of property, you will pay additional taxes on that property. Typically, this is a percentage of the assessed value of the property and the buildings on it. The higher the value, the higher the taxes.

Employment Taxes

You got a job. Yay! Your employer takes taxes out to pay the government. Boo! But you like the fact that you have roads to travel on to get to work. Meh?

That is the world of taxes, and every April 15th every working citizen has to file paperwork with the state and federal governments to prove that you are paying enough, to get money back if you paid too much, or to (gulp) pay more because you didn't have enough money taken out of your paycheck each pay period.

When you start a job, you should be asked to fill out a form that looks like the one below:

------------------------------ Separate here and give Form W-4 to your employer. Keep the top part for your records. ------------------------------

Form **W-4** Department of the Treasury Internal Revenue Service	**Employee's Withholding Allowance Certificate** ▶ Whether you are entitled to claim a certain number of allowances or exemption from withholding is subject to review by the IRS. Your employer may be required to send a copy of this form to the IRS.	OMB No. 1545-0074 **2017**

1	Your first name and middle initial	Last name		2	Your social security number

Home address (number and street or rural route)	3 ☐ Single ☐ Married ☐ Married, but withhold at higher Single rate. Note: If married, but legally separated, or spouse is a nonresident alien, check the "Single" box.
City or town, state, and ZIP code	4 If your last name differs from that shown on your social security card, check here. You must call 1-800-772-1213 for a replacement card. ▶ ☐

5	Total number of allowances you are claiming (from line **H** above **or** from the applicable worksheet on page 2)	**5**	
6	Additional amount, if any, you want withheld from each paycheck	**6**	$
7	I claim exemption from withholding for 2017, and I certify that I meet **both** of the following conditions for exemption.		
	• Last year I had a right to a refund of **all** federal income tax withheld because I had **no** tax liability, **and**		
	• This year I expect a refund of **all** federal income tax withheld because I expect to have **no** tax liability.		
	If you meet both conditions, write "Exempt" here . . . . ▶	**7**	

Under penalties of perjury, I declare that I have examined this certificate and, to the best of my knowledge and belief, it is true, correct, and complete.

Employee's signature
(This form is not valid unless you sign it.) ▶   Date ▶

8	Employer's name and address (Employer: Complete lines 8 and 10 only if sending to the IRS.)	9 Office code (optional)	10 Employer identification number (EIN)

For Privacy Act and Paperwork Reduction Act Notice, see page 2.   Cat. No. 10220Q   Form **W-4** (2017)

A W-4 form, as this is called, is how your employer knows how much money they should 'withhold' out of your paycheck, and forward to the government in the form of payroll taxes. You will fill out many forms like this in your lifetime, and the forms come with instructions on how to calculate how much money, or 'deductions', you should claim.

For most unmarried people, the safest bet is to claim one deduction – themselves. This likely will mean that you will get some money back at the end of the year, and worst case, not have to pay the IRS much more. If you have any questions about this, speak to your parents or a trusted friend who understands taxes.

Filing Tax Forms

Although you can spend money on software programs like TurboTax, most first-time workers don't need to do that, as your taxes are likely very simple. The easiest way is too look online for free tax applications that guide you through the process to file your federal taxes online. Most of these sites will charge you a small amount to also submit your state taxes (you will need to do both!). Here's a basic timeline:

1. In January or February, you should receive a W2 form from your employer. That's all you need to get your taxes done. If you don't receive them by mid-February, ask where they are.

2. Search online for one of the free tax sites.

3. Enter in your information into the site, and it will calculate whether you should get money back, or if you owe anything. Sometimes it works out so you don't owe, and don't get anything back. That is tax nirvana!

4. If you owe money, you can submit and pay at any time up to April 15th at 12 midnight.

5. If you are getting money back, you might want to go ahead and submit early, so the cash is in your hand ASAP.

6. Decide whether you want to simply pay for submitting your state taxes in the same way (it's usually about $15) or do them manually. Make sure you submit these no later than April 15th as well.

EXERCISE 8 — TAX QUIZ

1. **Why do we pay taxes?**

2. **What types of taxes will you likely pay in the next few years?**

3. **When are income taxes due?**

Important! Different Types of Employment

It is very important to understand how you are being paid when working, because if you don't know what you are signing up for, it can lead to having to pay unexpected taxes.

- ❑ **Regular employee, full-time (W4)** – This is a full-time job (38-40 hours a week) where you are either paid salary (a fixed rate) or hourly for the hours you actually work. Taxes are taken out.

- ❑ **Regular employee, part-time (W4)** – This is a part-time job (less than 38 hours) where you are either paid a salary or hourly for hours actually worked. Taxes are taken out.

- ❑ **Temporary employee (W4)** – This is job of a specific duration, a few weeks, or a few months, where you are either paid a salary or hourly for hours actually worked. Taxes are taken out.

- ❑ **Contract employee (1099)** – This is different! A contract employee, or an independent contractor, does not have taxes taken out, and so you must pay your own taxes in April. Many people work this way, and that's fine, but many unscrupulous (or ignorant) employers hire what should be part-time regular or temporary employees as contractors. Why? Because it's cheaper for them as they don't have to pay payroll taxes. But it is typically illegal.

- ❑ **Internships (should be W4)** – This is also different! By law, an unpaid internship must have a documented 'educational benefit' and be of a specific duration. Paid internships must also be of a specific duration, and must be documented as a W4. Because you are learning, you cannot (or should not) be considered to be a contractor.

By federal law, contractors should:

- ❑ Have all of the requisite skills to do a given job (meaning very little training)
- ❑ Make his or her own hours to work (meaning no set schedule)
- ❑ Never have business cards, attend staff meetings, or in any way do a 'regular' job type activity.

If you are being paid as a contractor, and you believe you are a temporary or part-time employee, talk to your manager. If they deny doing anything wrong, talk to a trusted friend or parent to see if you should report them to the IRS.

1. **Why does your employment type or status make a difference?**

2. **What type of employment should you watch out for?**

3. **What are two important things that make a contractor a contractor?**

Financial Extra Credit!

For those students who want to know a bit more about personal finances, keep reading to learn about finances you may need to know more about in the future.

Investments and Investment Types

If you should be so lucky that you have money at the end of each month, and you can invest it, or if you come into a large sum of money from an inheritance or another source, you should think about investing your money. You can keep your money in a savings account or money market account, but many people choose to use another type of investment instrument. There are many, many types of investments, but below are the most common types. Remember to always speak with your parents, a trusted friend, or a certified financial advisor before making any investments.

Stocks – Stocks are a unit of ownership in a company that are made available to the public for purchase. Companies that sell stocks are called 'publicly-held companies' and companies that do not sell stock are called 'privately-held companies.' Some company stock does very well, and some does very poorly, and buying and selling stock is considered to be a high-risk investment strategy, meaning that you can lose a great deal of money by investing in stock.

Bonds – Bonds are usually loans made by a government agency, such as a city, a county, or a state, to finance one or more endeavors. For example, a city may issue a bond in the amount of $1M to pay for school upgrades. Investors can purchase one or more shares of this bond, with the intention of being paid back the investment along with interest. Most governmental agencies will pay back these loans on time, but there is a risk that they will not. Some bonds are guaranteed, which means that the bank who has funded the city's loan will pay you even if the city cannot.

Mutual Funds – Mutual funds are a way to invest in the stock market with less risk of loss. Money that you invest in a mutual fund is pooled with other investors' cash, and is used to purchase a variety of stocks, bonds, and other financial instruments. Some mutual funds do very well, some not as well – it depends on the overall economy, the stock market, and the person or institution who is managing the mutual fund. Before investing in a money market account, ask to see what the 'track record' of that account has been for the last several years. This will give you an idea (though not a promise) of how well the money market account will do in the future.

401K, IRA, or SEP – These are different types of retirement savings accounts that allow you to save money tax-free for use when you retire. You cannot touch this money until retirement, but these are excellent ways to save for that day. If your employer has a matching fund, make sure to participate in it! The earlier you start, the more interest will accrue over time.

Charitable Contributions and Donations

Many people give money, services, or items to churches, homeless shelters, and other non-profit agencies such as United Way, The Sierra Club, or The Salvation Army. Most of these contributions or donations (if from a legitimate non-profit, or 503(c) company) can be deducted from your income tax, so save your receipts! So, instead of throwing out those blue jeans you never wear because they are too short, donate them to Goodwill, save the receipt, and you can deduct their value from your income tax. Either visit the IRS's website for more information or speak to whoever prepares your taxes to learn how you can reduce your taxes a bit this way.

Estate Planning

Let's say you've done everything right – you've spent your money wisely, you've saved money and invested it, you've bought a car, maybe a house, and have money in the bank. Once you have any sort of assets (the stuff you own are called assets), you need to think about who will get those assets when you die.

Now, the problem here is that most people in their teens and 20s, or even in their 30s, think that they will not die any time soon. And by and large, they are right. But, what if they do? Or, what happens if they are in a serious accident and cannot make any of their own decisions any longer?

The long and short of it is that by the time you have about $20,000 or more in assets, you should consider estate planning, which simply means drawing up a set of legal documents with a lawyer that describes:

❑ Who gets your money and your stuff when you die (a Will or Living Will, which may require setting up a Living Trust, which helps to alleviate the taxes your benefactors will pay on whatever they inherit from you when you die)

❑ Who will be responsible for making decisions for you if you cannot do so yourself (Durable Power of Attorney)

❑ Whether or not you want to be kept alive on life support, even if you are in a vegetative state, and there is no hope for you surviving without ongoing and constant medical supervision (Advance Directive)

Once you create an estate plan, you will likely need to update it on a fairly regular basis, and certainly when any major event happens, such as when you purchase a new home (more assets), you have children (more people to give things to), or if you get divorced (less people to give things to!). Note that while you can do your own estate planning by using a book or program (such as those offered by Nolo Press), many people prefer to hire a special lawyer to help them with this. Some such lawyers will not only prepare the original paperwork for you, but will also give you electronic forms so that you can update the paperwork yourself should your assets or situation change.

EXERCISE 10— EXTRA CREDIT QUIZ

1. **What is the difference between stock and a mutual fund?**

2. **Why would younger people want to make charitable contributions?**

3. **Why would younger people want to contribute to a 401k or an IRA?**

SECTION 5

HOME SWEET HOME

Finding the Right Home for You

There are many thing to consider when searching for a new home. We'll go through a series of questions that you can ask yourself in order to find a place that suits your needs and feels safe for you.

What Is My Budget?

You may have a budget for rent that is $500 a month or you may have a budget of $5000 a month. You must decide on what you can afford based on your own finances before you start looking for a place to live. When applying for apartments, you will often be asked to prove your income by asking to provide the name of your employer, how long you've been working with that company, and to confirm your pay by providing two or three months' worth of pay stubs. If you do not have these things then you may be asked to provide a bank statement proving that you have approximately 4 months rent available.

Your budget will in part determine where you will live and what size home you will be able to afford. You may be looking for a room in a boarding house, an apartment with one or two housemates, a studio, one bedroom, or full house.

Location, Location, Location

Do you want to be able to walk to school? Live near a market? Live in the country? Be near public transportation so that you can get to work without too much hassle? Make a list of what you need near you, or even what you'd like to be far away from (noise on a Saturday night, perhaps?). This list will help you find an area that will be a good fit for you.

People: Can't Live with 'Em ... Or Can You?

How do you feel about living with other people? People with less income may need to live with housemates until they are earning more money, so you may need to consider who you might want to live with. It also has some impact on what sort of housing you are looking for. Living in an apartment with another person who works all the time and keeps to him/herself might be perfect for you. But living in an apartment with a roommate who loves to stay up late gaming and partying may not be a good fit.

The Art Is in the Details

Do you have a cat, two dogs and a treadmill that are essential to your daily life? If so, you're likely going to have a more difficult time finding a place to live than someone without pets and large equipment.

So check: does the house or apartment you're interested in allow pets and have enough room for your treadmill?

Really take some time to consider what is essential to your well-being, and what is nice to have. Do you love to bake but the kitchen is dysfunctional? Do you want to be able to smoke/drink but the owners of the house don't allow it? What about guests? Can you tolerate loud music late at night? Do you own giant furniture? Can you live in a place without a lot of sunlight? That has a lot of stairs? Think about your routines and what routines are essential to your happiness in life. Keep all of these things in mind when looking at a place.

EXERCISE 1 — WHERE DO YOU WANT TO LIVE?

Take some time to list the things you <u>must</u> have in a new home:

1. _____

2. _____

3. _____

4. _____

Now, list things that are nice to have:

1. _____

2. _____

3. _____

4. _____

Be Flexible

As you have probably guessed, it may not be possible for you to get everything you want for the amount of money you can afford. This is true with most everyone, so don't feel alarmed. This is likely your first place away from your parents, not your last!

Go back through your lists above, and circle three things that are absolutely non-negotiable. This will help you find the perfect place. Maybe you find a place that is $400/month, but doesn't have any parking, but everything else is perfect, but it's a sketchy part of town and doesn't feel safe. Or maybe you find out that the closest parking is a block and a half away, but other than that, you like the place. Keep in mind what you can and cannot live with when searching for a home. Everyone is different, and what meets your must-haves (or close) is what we're looking for.

Resources for House Hunting

People find homes using a variety of methods:

- ❑ **Word of mouth** – You might hear of someone who is looking for a roommate in an existing home, either an apartment or a house. Or, a group of friends might go in together to rent a new place together. These are great ways to find housing as you will know the people up front.

- ❑ **College bulletin boards** – Another good way to find a place to live is to look on college bulletin boards in the area you wish to live. Even if you're not a student, this might be a good method.

- ❑ **Craigslist** – Yes, there are a lot of crazy people on Craigslist, but it is still one of the best ways to find shared living quarters, whether it's a house or an apartment. It's a good idea to go visit these places with a trusted friend or family member.

- ❑ **Apartment hunting sites** – There are many sites that list apartments for rent, where you can search using the zipcode of the location you wish to move to. These can be great if you are looking for an apartment in a big complex. Most smaller units cannot afford to list on these sites because they are expensive, but they are worth looking at. Simply search the internet for 'apartment sites' and you'll come up with several.

Checking out a Potential Apartment

So let's say you've answered an ad off of Craigslist about an apartment that sounds great. You've set up an appointment to see the space. Here are some helpful hints.

- ❑ Bring that list you made for yourself with the top 'must haves'.
- ❑ Bring a list of questions. Ask about noise, the other tenants, rules about the space, how food and meals are handled, who does the housecleaning, what utilities are included if any, and so forth.
- ❑ Bring a buddy!!! Bring a friend, parent or sibling who you trust to be professional when you visit a home. You are meeting a stranger off the internet – you have no idea who he/she is. Likewise, you are a stranger to them and it is important to give a good impression. Remember to be safe and let others know where you are going and when. Bringing a buddy will also give you someone to bounce ideas off of and a second pair of eyes to get an impression of the people, location and space itself.
- ❑ Evaluate how the place held up against your 'musts' and fill out an application if appropriate.

EXERCISE 2 — GOOD HOUSING QUIZ

1. **Where are some places you can look for housing?**

2. **What types of things will you want to know about a potential roommate?**

3. **What might happen if you are too picky about housing?**

4. **What type of things might you personally need to consider when looking for housing?**

Starting a New Household

Much of this training covers how to start a new household – what you will need to do to take care of yourself, what you will need to have in your home, and what to do when things go awry. This section deals mostly with the intricacies of procuring the housing itself. Renting an apartment is not difficult to do, but it is a very important step, so read this section carefully. Also, remember that when you rent an apartment, you will be expected to pay:

❑ **First month's rent** – Obviously. Rent is always paid in advance.

❑ **Last month's rent** – Just in case you move suddenly, or fall behind in your rent, you will likely be expected to put down a security deposit, which is typically one month's rent. You will use this last month's rent for your last month after you give 30 days (or more) notice that you plan on moving. You may be entitled to the interest that this money accrues while you are a tenant, depending on what state you live in. Check your local renters laws for more information.

❑ **Cleaning deposit** – You will likely be asked to give an amount of money to the landlord to hold until you leave the apartment which will cover cleaning costs in the event you leave the apartment trashed and the landlord has to pay to have it cleaned. You may be entitled to the interest that this money accrues while you are a tenant. Check your local renters laws for more information.

❑ **Pet or other deposit** – Some landlords will ask for an additional deposit if you have a pet or for other circumstances, such as a waterbed to cover the costs, in the event that extra cleaning or repairs need to be made.

It's important to note that whether or not you get any of these deposits back depends on how well you take care of the apartment while you live there. You cannot expect to get anything back if you never clean the place, let your dog pee in the corners, and gouge the walls with your furniture. The landlord is required to give you back your deposits if you leave the apartment in the same condition as when you rented it, minus what is called normal wear and tear.

In other words, if the carpet was only in decent shape when you rented the apartment, and after five years it has worn out in places just from normal foot traffic, you are not responsible for the cost of the carpet. If, however, the carpet was in decent shape originally, and your fish tank has repeatedly leaked on it, causing it to be stained and damaged, expect to pay for the damage.

Legal Documents to Understand

This section contains a few legal documents that pertain to rentals and leases. Before you sign any rental or lease agreement, understand that they are **legally-binding documents**. This means that with a few and very rare exceptions, you must abide by the agreement if you sign it. Therefore, you must understand and be willing to fulfill all of the conditions of the agreement.

The good news is that the landlord must also comply with the agreement, and if s/he does not, you have legal recourse against him or her. Here are the documents included in this section – all of them are real legal documents, but may or may not be exactly the same as the ones you are asked to sign.

- ❑ **Residential Rental Application** – This document is a typical example of an application to rent an apartment. Landlords have the right to review your information, your credit rating, and other personal information about you before deciding whether or not to let you rent an apartment. That's why it's call an application, and not an agreement. However, if you sign this document you do not have the option of cancelling the application. It is assumed that you will rent the apartment if your application is accepted. Remember, a rental is generally a month-to-month agreement. That means that you must give 30 days' notice before you move out. It also means that the landlord can ask you to move out in 30 days – if they have one of a few legal reasons, like they need the apartment to live in themselves.

- ❑ **Residential Lease Guaranty** – Frequently, young people do not have any or much credit history, which makes some landlords nervous about renting to them. This can create a chicken and egg situation, where you need to rent to build credit, but you can't rent until you have credit. In situations like this, you can ask (or the landlord will ask you) to have someone, usually a parent, sign a guaranty for you. What this means is that if you cannot pay (or simply choose not to pay, if you're a jerk!) the person listed as your 'guarantor' will pay your rent for you until the end of the agreement.

- ❑ **Rental Property Inventory and Condition Form** – This is an excellent form to use when you move into an apartment. It lists pretty much every aspect of an apartment, from cupboards, to stove, to carpets, to light fixtures. Use this list to go through every room in the apartment and check everything on this list to make sure it is in good working order. If it is not, or if there is any wear or tear, make a note of it on this list. When you have filled out the entire list, sign it, make a copy of it, and send the original by certified or registered mail to the landlord. S/he should sign it and mail it back, but if not, keep your receipt of the certified/registered mail along with your original in case there is any dispute when you move out.

❑ **Rental Property Inspection Checklist** – This is a checklist used by many landlords that tells you specifically what you must do to get your cleaning deposit back when you move out.

Setting up Services after Moving In

❑ **Mail** – You can have your mail forwarded to your new address. You can do so in a couple of different ways. You can go to the post office, pick up a packet, and fill it out to have all of your mail forwarded to your new address. For a fee ($1.00) you can change it online at this address: https://moversguide.usps.com. Be careful as there are a lot of scams out there that offer to change your address for you and charge you $10-$20 to do so. Make sure that you go to the USPS website and that USPS is in the URL.

❑ **Gas and Electricity** – These may be part of your rent, so check with your landlord if they are paid or not. If not, you will need to sign up for services. Depending on where you live, gas and electricity may be bundled together or may be handled separately. In some parts of the country, natural gas is not available, and heating may be done by oil. Speak to a trusted friend or family member about setting up utilities in your area.

❑ **Water and Garbage** – These may be part of your rent, so check with your landlord if they are paid or not. If not, you will need to sign up for services. And like power, water and garbage may be bundled together or may be separate. Speak to a friend or relative, or check with the city in which you live to find out how these are handled and how you sign up. These are frequently handled by the local city or county. Check the website for your town to find out whom to contact.

❑ **Phone, Cable and Internet** – Don't forget to contact your local internet and/or cable provider for new service, and if you plan on having a land line in your home, make sure to contact the phone company as well. Many providers have 'bundles' where you get a better deal if you buy all services from one company. Shop and compare!

❑ **Other Accounts** – Update your address information for credit cards, bank accounts, schools and cell service.

1. What are some of the things you need to pay before you move into a new home?

2. What should you do before you sign any contracts or other documents?

3. What services might you have to set up in your new home?

4. If you are the only person listed on the contract, who is ultimately responsible for paying the rent and for any damages?

What to Do If Something Goes Wrong

In every life, a little rain must fall, and renting apartments or houses and having roommates sometimes means that a little rain will fall on you. Here are a few tips on what to do if things go wrong.

If any of these things happen to you, your first line of defense is to contact your city or township and ask if they (or the county) has a renters board that helps with issues between landlords and tenants. Most areas have these, and they can guide you on the specific laws and remediations in place in your location. The information here is current and applicable for most areas in California at the time of publication.

Something Breaks in the Apartment

Things break. It's as simple as that. The garbage disposal will stop working on Thanksgiving, and the toilet will overflow on Hanukkah. When something breaks in your apartment, you have three choices:

- ❑ Try to fix it yourself (often the best option if possible)
- ❑ Call the landlord and have him/her fix it (sometimes takes a while)
- ❑ Call a repair person, have it fixed, and hope the landlord will pay you back ('hope' being the operative word here)

If you can, the best thing to do with simple problems is to fix it yourself. Use a plunger to try to unclog the toilet, or Drano to unclog the sink. If the toilet or sink repeatedly clog up, tell your landlord, because it may mean that there is a larger clog further down the line, and it needs to be professionally cleaned out. See the section on *Home Maintenance* for more information.

If it's something that you can't reasonably fix, then you'll either need to call the landlord or call a repair person. Deciding which step to take depends on your relationship with the landlord, and your past experience with him/her. Most property owners do not want you to get something fixed without their prior permission because they have their own repair people they like to use. So, the best bet is generally to call the landlord immediately, tell them what the problem is (calmly!) and ask them when you can expect to have the repair made. Generally, local laws state that the landlord has a few days to get the repair done, unless it is causing a dangerous situation (such as a gas leak, or no heat in the winter, or no electricity – all of which must be fixed immediately).

Sometimes, the landlord will agree to let you hire a repairperson to fix the problem, and then will reimburse you for the costs. However, without something in writing, you do run a risk that the landlord will later say that s/he never gave you permission – you only have a verbal agreement, and cannot prove that s/he okayed it. If at all possible, try to get the landlord to agree to the repair via email – that way, you have a written record of the agreement.

An important note: if whatever broke did so because you were doing something silly, like flushing wads of cash down the toilet, YOU are responsible for the repair. The landlord is only responsible for 'reasonable repairs' – that is to say, things that broke because of normal wear and tear. If you are abusing the apartment or its fixtures, expect to pay for the repairs yourself. It's only fair.

The Landlord Refuses to Fix Something

Yes, sometimes landlords can be complete dillweeds and either flat out refuse to fix something or take so darn long in making the repairs that it makes your life miserable. There are renters laws that protect against this sort of thing, but it doesn't necessarily mean that landlords obey the law all the time.

In California, if the landlord refuses to make the repairs in a reasonable time, then you can:

- ❑ Have the repair made yourself and deduct the amount from your rent the following month
- ❑ Choose to move out (breaking your rental agreement)

There are some major caveats here. First, the definition of 'reasonable time' is not set in stone. Assume the worst, and for repairs that don't impact your health or safety, assume that this means 30 days. For repairs that do impact your health or safety (toilet backing up, sink clogged, heat not working in the winter) you can assume this to mean 48 hours.

Next, if you do make repairs yourself, first contact the landlord, preferably by phone and by letter, and inform him that you are going to make the repair and deduct the cost from your rent. This frequently will cause the landlord to get off his/her butt and fix it. If not, that's fine – go ahead and schedule the repair. Be aware, however, that you can only legally deduct repairs costing less than one month's rent. So, if you pay $950 a month, and the repair costs $375, you're fine. If the repair costs $1,000, however, you can only 'deduct' $949, and may be out $51.

If the repairs are huge and the landlord is stalling and stalling, you have the right to break the rental agreement and move out. Do so by stating in writing why you are breaking the lease (the porch collapsed, the entire plumbing system is not working, one or more kitchen appliances are not working, etc.) and move on to a better living situation.

For more information, ALWAYS check with your city's or state's renters protection agency. In California, you can find information at http://www.dca.ca.gov/publications/landlordbook index.shtml.

EXERCISE 4 — WHAT TO DO IF SOMETHING GOES WRONG

1. What should you do if something small goes wrong in your home, like a stopped up drain?

2. What should you do if something bigger happens, like sewage backing up in the shower?

3. What should you always understand before you put pressure on your landlord to make repairs?

Neighbors Gone Amuck

Sometimes apartment buildings feel like zoos, and the neighbors act like animals. Parties late into the night, garbage strewn all over, neighbors parking in your parking spot, kids screaming at all hours of the day or night.

First off, remember that living in an apartment building is not the same as living in a detached home. You are in closer quarters with your neighbors, and some noise and inconvenience is to be expected. You have to ask yourself if you are being unreasonable about your expectations. Kids play, and sometimes they make noise. They have the right to do that. People cook, and sometimes the smells waft into your apartment. People have the right to cook and eat pretty much anything they choose. People have friends over or throw parties, and sometimes they talk louder than normal. Again, this is their right as long as they obey the 'quiet hours'.

The bottom line is that you need to be sure that you are not being a sourpuss before you make a complaint. Here are some things that you do have the right to be annoyed or alarmed by:

- ❑ **Parties that go on past 10 or 11 pm** — This is the 'quiet enjoyment' clause in the rental agreement. Usually apartment managers will require quiet at 10 pm, and the local city ordinance will require it by 11 pm. The best course of action here is to try to wait it out until 11 pm, and if it doesn't break up by then, then knock on the door, and *very politely* ask them to keep it down because you need to sleep. If they are complete jerks, don't get mad, just go home and call the police on the non-emergency line (in the phonebook or on your city's website). The police will come out and break up the party. Then, the next day, report it to your landlord. If it continues to be a problem, write a letter to the landlord that states that s/he is breaking your rental agreement by not taking care of the problem and if it is not rectified in 30 days, you will move out.

- ❑ **People blocking your parking spot** — Call your landlord and complain. If your car is in your parking spot and someone is blocking you so that you cannot get out, call the police and have the car towed, and complain to the landlord.

- ❑ **Fighting or domestic violence** — If you hear a fight in your apartment complex, especially if there are children involved or someone is being abused physically, call 911 **immediately**. Do not get involved, but make sure the police do!

- ❑ **Illegal activity** — This includes theft and obvious drug dealing and prostitution. It does not include someone having a pet in a no-pet apartment complex, someone taking nudie pictures, or someone shouting for a few minutes. Worry about the big picture stuff, and let the rest of the stuff go. Call the police, but don't get involved personally.

The Roommate from Hell

One of the great joys of having a roommate is getting to known him/her. Even if you have been friends for decades, you will learn more about people by living with them than you have ever known before. They may hum in their sleep. Insist on eating pancakes with anchovy paste. Chew their toenails off in the living room when your girlfriend is over. You laugh now, but these are all true stories.

Living with human foibles (which we all have) is one thing, but some roommates cross the line. Maybe they never pay rent on time. Or refuse to ever clean up and are a complete slob. Maybe they party until 3 am every night, so that you can't sleep.

What you can do depends on how the rental/lease agreement is set up. Did you sign the rental agreement, and your roommate co-signed? (Usually, only one person is the 'main' renter, because the landlord wants to know who to go after in case of a dispute.)

If you are the main renter, you can work to evict your roommate:

- ❑ **Talk to your roommate** – Don't yell, don't threaten. Set up a time to have a 'town meeting' and list out, calmly, the things that are not working for you. If your roommate was totally oblivious to what s/he has been doing that is driving you nuts (which does happen), list out what you would like to do to fix the situation. Then, see how it goes. Don't expect perfection, because you won't get it. Remember, you have foibles, too. Compromise and forgive.

- ❑ **Send a letter to your roommate** – This may seem odd as you are living together, but sending a written letter that is dated and sent certified mail becomes a legal document that you can use later if need be to demonstrate that you talked about these issues and that the issues still remain. Again, write an organized, calm letter stating the issues. State that the roommate has agreed to change his/her behavior, but has not done so. List examples and state that your roommate has 30 days to change or you will ask him/her to move out.

- ❑ **Give them notice** – If after 30 days the behavior has not changed, send another letter giving the roommate 30 days to vacate the premises. State what will happen if s/he does not go on his/her own – specifically, that you will change the locks and remove all possessions and put them in the carport or some other location where the roommate can pick them up.

- ❑ **Follow up on the action** – You're done. Make sure to notify your landlord that you have had to have the premises re-keyed and give your landlord a key.

Don't forget to keep copies of ALL of the letters you sent in case the roommate takes legal action. You need a record of how you handled this case!

If you are the co-signer on the rental agreement, give 30 days notice stating exactly why you are moving out, and then do so. If you are the co-signer on a lease agreement, check the language very carefully to make sure that you can break the lease. In many cases, you will be able to do so, but if you need advice, get it. Check online for public assistance for renters for more information.

EXERCISE 5— NOT SO GOOD TIMES QUIZ

1. **What should you do if your neighbors have a loud party at 8 pm?**

2. **What should you do if your neighbors are still partying hard at 12 am?**

3. **What should you do if you suspect illegal activity in your housing complex or neighborhood, or suspect someone is being abused or hurt?**

Breaking the Rental/Lease Agreement

As you can see, there are a few legal ways that you can break a rental or lease agreement. If the landlord does not make good on his/her responsibilities in a timely fashion, you can move out. Yes, it's a pain, and yes, you may end up fighting over the deposits, but you'll be out of a nasty situation.

Similarly with a roommate, you may be able to break an agreement and get the heck out. Sometimes, this is the best course of action, so long as you protect yourself legally. Always check with the local authorities on your rights, as the laws surrounding renters protection change frequently.

Illegal Rent Increases

Another area where the law changes frequently is around what is called rent control – how frequently, and by how much, a landlord can increase your rent. These laws are set city by city, so depending on where you live, you will have different kinds or levels of protection. If you have a year-long lease, usually landlords can only increase your rent once a year, usually on the anniversary date of your moving in, and generally can only raise them by a certain percentage.

IMPORTANT NOTE: It is a good idea to look into the city laws that protect renters BEFORE making a decision on which city to rent an apartment in. Some cities have great protection, and others none at all. This may impact your decision!

EXERCISES 6— LEGAL REMEDIES QUIZ

1. Is there ever a time when you can legally break a lease and move out?

2. When can a landlord raise the rent? And by how much?

3. Do you have any legal remedies if the landlord refuses to make repairs in a timely fashion?

The Perfect Roommate

Finding the perfect roommate is about as impossible as finding the perfect mate. The reason for this is because none of us is perfect, and all of us are likely to annoy someone else at some point in our lives. And, depending on how picky or easygoing you are, the harder or easier it may be to find a suitable match. Read through this information to help you figure out what would be the perfect roommate for you.

❑ **Think about what you want from a roommate.** Do you want someone you can basically ignore, who is just there to help pay the bills, or do you want someone you actually like personally and may enjoy hanging out with?

❑ **Slob or clean or in-between?** There's nothing wrong morally with be a clean freak or a total slob, but you do need to be honest about your living habits and ask potential roommates about theirs. Ditto with things like cooking, partying, playing video games all night, having friends come over and stay, and so forth.

❑ **Make a list of the things that you absolutely could not stand in a roommate.** It should not have more than 2-5 items. If it does, you're probably being too picky. Next, compile a list of the things that would make a perfect roommate. Having similar lifestyles generally make for good roommates.

❑ **If at all possible, meet each potential roommate in person after you have connected via phone or email.** Meeting someone face to face will tell you a lot more about your compatibility than any other method. While you're chatting with them, ask yourself if you could live with this person.

❑ **Ask open-ended, not yes-no, questions, but be tactful**. For example, don't ask someone if s/he is a slob. Ask instead, "How do you feel about housework?" You'll get much better answers. You may also want to ask what the person likes to do for fun, rather than asking if they smoke weed or like to have kegger parties. By being open and honest yourself, you're more likely to get open and honest responses.

❑ **Ask for references before making a decision.** Be wary of folks who call you – you should get names and numbers of three to five different people who have known this person for at least two years, preferably longer. Ex-roommates are okay, family friends and teachers are great, friends are only so-so.

❑ **Finally, if it sounds too good to be true, it probably is.** There are lots of people out there who are happy to take your money and run. Be careful, use a trusted friend or family member to help you make decisions until you get the hang of it.

Getting Along with a Roommate

You've heard me say it before, but I'll say it again – no one, not even you – is perfect! You need to find a midway point when living with others between being taken advantage of and controlling everything that goes in within your domicile. Below are a set of rules you should follow, and maybe even ask your roommate to follow, to ensure you avoid the avoidable conflicts.

❑ **Talk it over** – If you are upset or angry about something your roommate is doing or not doing, the first step is to calm down a bit, and then talk it over. Be honest, but be tactful. Don't raise your voice, don't make threats, just state what your issues are.

❑ **Respect privacy** – If what is bugging you has something to do with your roommate's personal life and it does not directly impact you, is not illegal, or does not put you in harm's way, let it go. Live and let live. If your roommate starts sleeping with girls after he told you he was gay, it's really none of your business.

❑ **Avoid TMI** – By the same token, you need to know what your own boundaries are, and avoid the Too-Much-Information syndrome. Even close friends have limits on how much they want to know about each other. So, if what's bothering you is that your roommate doesn't seem interested in your long stories about your infected toe while he's eating dinner, consider talking to someone else about what's going on in your life. Also, if you've had a crappy day, you don't have the right to take it out on your roommate. Tell your roommate you're in a crappy mood, go to your room, and call a friend to rant and rave.

❑ **Agree to disagree** – It's okay for people who live together to have different viewpoints. In fact, it happens all the time. So what if the two of you can't agree on which was the best Star Wars movie? It's not worth spending the energy engaging in conflict over. And don't always try to have the last word. It's silly.

What Roommates Fight About

People who live together can and do fight about everything. Frequently, a roommate gets upset because they do not feel they are getting the respect they believe they are entitled to — that personal boundaries are being crossed. How this actually manifests is usually in one of the following ways:

❏ **Space** — How much space are each of you taking up? Do you have your stuff strewn all over the bathroom? Is your computer equipment taking up the dining room? If you are paying equal rent, you should each have equal amounts of space. You don't need to get all weird about it, and put masking tape on the carpet to mark boundaries, but do try to be fair. Generally, apartments have separate space (bedrooms) and shared or common living space. Common living space should be that — common. Everyone gets to use it equally.

❏ **Safety** — It is reasonable to expect that you are safe — and that your possessions are safe — in your home. This means that the doors are locked, the windows are locked, and the people who have access to the inside of your apartment are people known to you and trusted by you. You do not have the right to give a house key to a friend that your roommate has never met without asking your roommate in advance, and vice versa. Having said that, if your roommate has a friend coming into to town and will be at work all week, ask yourself if it is such a big deal to let this friend stay. If you trust your roommate and have a good relationship, you can probably trust the friend. But if in doubt, say no.

❏ **Cleanliness** — You don't get to be a slob in the common areas of the living space unless your roommate is also a complete slob. You should have already had this conversation before you moved in together, right? Wash your own dishes, clean up your own mess, and don't leave your laundry in the washer or dryer for weeks on end.

❏ **Noise** — Ditto on noise. You don't get to blast your music at 4 am unless your roommate does not mind and it's not bugging anyone else. You also don't get to have a loud conversation on the telephone in the living room if your roommate is trying to watch TV. Take it into your bedroom.

❏ **Sex** — You don't get to use the common areas for sex unless you are certain that your roommate will not be coming home before you are finished. No one wants to walk in on you. It's embarrassing. Note that this also includes watching pornography (unless mutually acceptable to all roommates) and, um, personal gratification. Again, take it into your bedroom.

❏ **Personal Property** — Is just that. Personal. You never, ever get to borrow something or use something if it is not yours unless you have explicit permission to do so. And then you give it right back and put it exactly where it was when you borrowed it; and if you used something up, you replace it right away. Period.

- ❑ **Common Property** – This is likely to include paper towels, toilet paper, cleaning supplies, and maybe food and drinks. Decide immediately how you will take care of this stuff. There is no one right answer, but the easiest is to each put in some money once a month into a jar, and agree to use it for a set list of items that you both share.

- ❑ **Common Bills** – Same thing. Agree on how you will split utilities, garbage, phone bills, and so forth, then follow through.

- ❑ **Common Meals** – Some roommates like to share meals, which is a great way to cut down on cooking, cost, and clean up. However, you need to agree to who pays for what, who is cooking, and who is cleaning up.

In short, the best way to get along with a roommate is to always remember the Golden Rule – do unto others as you would have them do unto you. Be a grown up and don't be a dillweed!

EXERCISE 7— ROOMMATES!

1. **What kind of roommate do you think you'll be in terms of friendliness, helpfulness, cleanliness, and timeliness of paying bills?**

2. **What are your 'non-negotiables' in terms of what you can tolerate in a roommate?**

3. **What type of roommate do you want?**

4. **What kind of things do you think you might fight about with a roommate? What will drive you nuts?**

5. **How do you think you'll handle any disagreements before they get ugly?**

Home Maintenance

Whether you own or rent, you will need to learn home maintenance basics, if for no other reason than it always being faster (and usually cheaper) to fix something yourself than to have someone else do it for you. If you are a renter, most of this work will be done by your landlord, but you should still be on the lookout, and ask for any of the following to be addressed if necessary.

Maintenance is what you do to try to avoid repairs. It doesn't always work that way, because things still break, but if you keep your home in good repair, you'll save yourself time and money in repairs later.

The first place to start is to go through your home on a regular basis – at least once or twice a year – and check the following items:

- ❏ **Filters** – Remember to clean or replace furnace and air conditioner/air filters twice a year, or as needed. Check and clean the dryer vent, air conditioner, stove hood and room fans. Keep heating and cooling vents clean and free from furniture and draperies.

- ❏ **Doors/Hinges** – Make sure that all doors swing and lock properly, and are easy to open. If they aren't or if they are squeaking, spray them with lubricant like WD-40.

- ❏ **Electrical Outlets and Switches** – If you find one or more outlets or switches that don't work, call your landlord and ask them to make a repair. In the meantime, you can cover them with a piece of masking tape to remind yourself they are not working.

- ❏ **Safety Equipment** – Ensure that all smoke detectors, carbon monoxide detectors and fire extinguishers are in good working order. Replace batteries in appropriate devices as needed, or at least twice each year.

- ❏ **Refrigerator** – Make sure your refrigerator door seals are airtight. Test them by closing the door over a dollar bill. If you can pull the bill out easily, the latch may need to be adjusted or the seal may need to be replaced. In addition, if you have a coil-back refrigerator, vacuum the coils at least twice each year. Your refrigerator will run more efficiently with clean coils. Also, stock up! A full refrigerator uses less energy than an empty one.

- ❏ **Faucets** – Check for leaky faucets in the kitchen and bathroom(s). Replace washers as necessary.

- ❏ **Windows and Doors** – Seal drafty doors and windows. If you added up all of the small cracks where heating and cooling escapes from a home, it could be the same as having a window open. Replace seals as needed.

❑ **Siding and Paint** – Look for cracks and holes in house siding or paint. Replace caulk if necessary. A carpet knife can work well for cutting away old caulking from house siding. Slice down alongside it from both directions with the hook-like blade, then use the knife to lift out the old caulk bead intact. Patch holes, touch up paint inside and out.

❑ **Check for Pests** – Be on the look out for signs of critters who have moved in. Remove hornet nests by spraying them with hornet nest spray. Spray for ants and cockroaches. Call a pest control company to remove rats or mice if you find droppings.

Making Repairs

If you've gone through your home carefully, you'll likely find several quick and easy repairs that need to be done. Repairs generally require either taking something apart and putting it back together again, or simply putting something back together or filling or patching. This first section talks about adhesives used to glue things back together, which is often the simplest way to make a small repair. Later portions of this section describe how to make general repairs.

Repairs with Adhesives

The table below contains a listing of common repairs that can be made with adhesives. Be sure to read through the information before attempting to repair an item.

Item	Product	How To
Broken Ceramic or Glass	Elmer's ProBond China & Glass Cement is food and dishwasher-safe.	Lightly sand both edges. Wipe with a clean cloth, then coat one edge with glue. Press the pieces together. Apply masking tape across the glued joint as a clamp. Let set for three or more hours.
Small Breaks in Ceramic, Glass, or Plastic	A cyanoacrylate-based glue, like Scotch Super Glue Liquid Plus, creates an inflexible bond that resists moderate heat and moisture.	Coat one side of the break with a thin layer of glue. Fit the pieces together and hold firmly for 30 seconds. The adhesive will set fully in a minute or so.
Breaks in Wood	A polyurethane-based adhesive, like Gorilla Glue, is ideal for woodworking (it's also good for big ceramic, plastic, laminate, and stone repairs and projects). This type of glue withstands shock, heat, and moisture and can be sanded, painted, or stained. This glue is toxic!	For breaks in wooden items that don't come into contact with food, especially ones that need to withstand a large amount of stress (such as a loose chair leg or a tabletop that has separated from its base). Clamp or firmly secure the glued sections for one to two hours, depending on the size and the weight of the piece.
Breaks in Wood that Has Indirect Contact with Food	Nontoxic, odorless, and water-resistant, Titebond II Premium Wood Glue's FDA-approved for indirect contact with food.	For a break in a wooden cooking utensil, such as a handle that has snapped off a meat mallet. (No glue is advised for surfaces that touch food directly.) Apply glue to one surface only and let stand for a few minutes before joining the pieces. Clamp for 30 to 60 minutes.

Item	Product	How To
Breaks in Plastic	IPS Weld-On 16 Cement chemically welds the surfaces it touches.	For a break in a plastic object that needs to withstand a certain amount of wear and tear (such as a container with a cracked lid) or an object that is flexible. Apply to both pieces and wait 15 to 30 seconds for the glue to get tacky before joining. Align parts and hold together for about a minute, applying moderate pressure. The cement will set completely in 12 to 24 hours.
Tears in Fabric	Elmer's Craft Bond Fabric & Paper Glue is nontoxic and virtually invisible when dry. And the bond is flexible, which means it moves with the fabric.	For a tear in home-interior fabrics, curtains that need to be hemmed because they are too long, or trim that needs to be added to clothing, throw pillows, and lamps (not suitable if the bulb is more than 60 watts). Wash and dry the fabric before gluing. Test the glue in an inconspicuous spot to see if it stains (as it will with silk). Apply glue to one surface, then join and hold together for a few minutes. The glue sets completely in 24 hours.
Laminates	Duro All-Purpose Spray Adhesive is heat- and water-resistant, making it suitable for use in the kitchen or the bathroom.	For a veneer that has separated from its base materials, such as the 30-year-old Formica countertop that came with the house or the edging to inexpensive cabinet shelves and drawers. Apply a medium coat to both surfaces. Let set for one minute, then press the surfaces together. Apply pressure or a clamp for up to 5 minutes.

How to Reset a Circuit Breaker or Change a Fuse

One of the most common problems in a house or apartment is having the power go out. Before you call the power company, see if someone has accidentally 'tripped' the circuit breaker.

1. Locate your circuit breaker. It is usually outside in the back or side of the house, in the utility room, or in a closet.

2. Open the box, and look at the switches – those are the circuit breakers.

3. Look to see if one of the switches is in the midway position, neither ON nor OFF. If so, that is the breaker that got tripped.

4. Press the switch all the way to the OFF position, and leave it there for a count of three.

5. Press the switch all the way to the ON position, and check to see if your power has been restored. If not, call your power company.

Tools for the Garden

If you have a garden, you will need a few tools to keep it up. Here are some tips for what you'll need and how to pick them.

- ❑ **Try tools on for size.** You can't dig a hole in the aisle at Home Depot, but you should spend time handling tools, mimicking the actions you perform in the garden. If the tool feels too heavy, you risk injury; if the handle is too long or too big, it won't be comfortable. Look for D-shape handles on short-shafted tools, such as shovels and digging forks; they are easier on the wrists than other types of handles. If you buy over the Internet, make sure tools are returnable.

- ❑ **Opt for tools with wood or coated-metal handles,** which are strong but not too heavy. Ash and hickory are the most durable woods. Avoid Douglas fir, which is used for lesser-quality tools, and painted handles (paint is often used to disguise the use of inferior-quality wood). The closer and tighter the grain, the stronger the wood. Manufacturers make many confusing claims about quality, but the words "single forged," "solid socket," "carbon steel," "stainless steel," "tempered," and "epoxy coated" are all indicators of well-made tools. Tubular-steel and fiber-glass handles, used on professional tools, are generally too heavy and expensive for use by anyone but professional landscapers.

- ❑ **Store tools properly.** There's no need to trip over your garden implements. Long-handled tools can be hung neatly on a peg rack, which also protects edges from dulling. Short-handled tools can be stored in a garden bag that travels with you as you work. Keep the edges of spades and other tools from nicking and dulling by storing them off the floor. And make sure you keep them out of the rain.

- ❑ **Hand Rake:** For picking up piles of leaves and garden trash and gently removing debris from under and around plants without damaging roots or crowns.

- ❑ **Shears:** For trimming grass around tree trunks and shrubs, edging beds and paths, and cutting back ornamental grasses and clumps of perennials.

- ❑ **Scissors:** For deadheading (removing dead flowers); cutting soft stemmed plants, such as herbs; pruning small or delicate plants; snipping twine; and thinning perennials.

- ❑ **Hand Pruner:** For cutting branches less than ¾ inch thick, cutting back clumps of perennials, cutting larger flowers, and scoring and slicing root balls before planting.

- ❑ **Hand Weeder:** The thin, sharp blade removes shallow-rooted weeds; the long handle lets you reach far into beds.

1. **What are a few of the things you should check your house/apartment for every so often?**

2. **What type of things do you think might wear out in an apartment that you either would need to fix yourself or call the landlord to repair?**

3. **List the type of tools and materials you think you might need to have on hand for typical home maintenance.**

Cleaning Basics

No one likes cleaning. At least, no one I know. But, pretty much everyone I know enjoys a clean home. Therefore, most folks have two options:

1. Learn to clean quickly and effectively and **regularly**

2. Hire someone else to clean for you

There is nothing wrong with hiring a cleaning service. However, they are not free, so you have to determine whether or not you can afford a service. Also remember that cleaning services are not 'pick up and straighten' services. If you leave a huge mess for your cleaning service, they will spend a lot of extra time (and your money) picking crap up, and they won't know where it goes, which means you may spend months locating your belongings. So, you still should pick up all of the dirty laundry, dishes, etc. before you have a cleaning service over.

IMPORTANT NOTE: If you want any sort of romantic life whatsoever, you will need to have a clean home. There is little that is less appealing than a person whose home looks like a set for a horror movie.

Start with a Plan

The most effective way to clean your home is to know what you plan on doing and when. You can either decide to spend a larger portion of one day doing your cleaning, or you can do a little cleaning each day; it doesn't make any difference. What does make a difference is that you stay on top of the work. If you let housecleaning go untouched for several weeks, you will feel absolutely overwhelmed by the work.

Basic Supplies

Here are the very basic items you will need to keep your house clean:

- ❏ Clorox or other brand cleaning wipes
- ❏ Windex or window cleaning solution
- ❏ All-surface cleaner
- ❏ SoftScrub or other cleanser
- ❏ Dust wipes
- ❏ Sponges
- ❏ Paper towels
- ❏ Mop or Swiffer
- ❏ Toilet brush
- ❏ Vacuum, electric broom and/or carpet cleaner
- ❏ Broom and dust pan
- ❏ Garbage bags, both liners for the trash cans, and large (3 gallon sized) for major clean ups

EXERCISE 9— CLEANING QUIZ!

1. **How often should you plan on cleaning your home or room? Why?**

2. **What type of supplies will you need to have in your home to keep it clean?**

3. **What happens to your romantic life if you're a slob?**

10 Quick Tips

1. Don't let the house get so trashed that cleaning it is overwhelming. Stay on top of it, even if it means cleaning just one room each week.

2. Keep cleaning wipes in the bathrooms and in the kitchen. Every few days, take a wipe in the bathroom, wipe down the sink, the counters, and then the toilet seat and the toilet rim. Use a toilet brush in the toilet bowl every few days and it will never get grungy.

3. If you 'shed' when you brush your hair (you'll notice piles of your hair in the bathroom if you do – yuck) go outside when brushing your hair. Brush it vigorously to loosen and remove all of the dead hair, saving you time next time you clean.

4. Use a cleaning schedule and post it on the fridge. One has been included at the end of this section.

5. Make a plan of action before you start to clean. Know what you plan on cleaning, what you will need to clean, and how long you plan on cleaning.

6. Always have your cleaning supplies on hand.

7. Keep your cleaning supplies all in one location. Choose a place that is large enough to hold all of your cleaning supplies, and keep it well-supplied (add items you are low on or out of to your shopping list).

8. Before you start to clean, pick up and straighten the room. You can't clean with crap lying all over the room. Put things back where they belong, recycle them, or throw them out.

9. As you pick up all the stuff, make a mental note to stop leaving stuff lying around! Don't leave crap lying everywhere. When you're done eating the popcorn, take the bowl out to the kitchen, and wash it or put it in the dishwasher. When you've finished reading the paper, pick it up and recycle it. Don't rationalize leaving it spread out all over the floor by saying someone else may want to read it.

10. Play some of your favorite music when you clean, or listen to music on your phone. Cleaning goes much faster when you have some motivational music.

1. **What tricks will you try in the next month at home?**

2. **Why do you think it's a good idea to get into the habit of cleaning before you move out?**

Attack!

Keep these points in mind when you clean:

1. Pick a room, any room. Start by picking up all of the trash, taking all the dishes and dirty laundry out, and putting them where they belong.

2. Start at the top. Dust doorways, then surfaces, then floors. Dust settles.

3. In the kitchen, attack the stovetop and sink before doing the counters. The grease and grime that accumulate in your sponge will just spread around if you don't clean the grungiest stuff first. And don't forget to thoroughly clean your sponge between jobs. Better yet, throw gross stuff out, and use a clean one.

4. If you're cleaning your oven, first check to see if it is a self-cleaning type. If so, secure the lock and set the controls to self-clean. In a few hours, you can open it and wipe it out with a damp sponge.

5. In the bathroom, liberally spray the bathtub/shower with bathroom cleaner and let it soak while you clean the rest of the bathroom. The cleaning agents will start to cut through the scale and soap scum while you clean, making your job easier.

6. You can't clean with dirty water, dirty sponges, or dirty towels. You're just spreading the dirt around. Change the water, clean out the sponge (or get a new one), and use a new paper towel.

7. Don't try to mop over loose dirt. Vacuum or sweep first if there is a lot of junk on the floor, or your mop will get disgustingly clogged up with hair.

8. Don't forget to wipe down cabinet fronts and drawers. They get food and fingerprints on them.

9. In the kitchen and in the bathroom, it won't kill you to get down on your knees with a damp paper towel and scoop/mop up the grunge in the corners BEFORE you mop.

Pigsty City

Okay, so you had the best intentions for keeping your apartment habitable, but things got out of hand and now it is just too gross for words. What to do? Here are some suggestions:

- ❑ **Hire help**. Find a cleaning service in the phone book or on the internet and have the professionals come in. Expect to pay a premium if the house is really bad, but hey, it's better than having your apartment condemned by the health department.

- ❑ **Enlist help**. If you have some really good friends or family members who are willing to help you, make a party out of it. Have everybody over, order a bunch of pizza, and get to work. Having help makes the job go much faster, and having friends and family members will force you to part with things like stacks of newspapers that you will never use again.

- ❑ **Just do it**! One room at a time, 'de-grungify'. Make one room absolutely spotless, and then pledge to keep it clean. Next week, work on another room, and do the same. In a month or so, the place will be back to normal.

EXERCISE 11— HOUSECLEANING AS A HABIT QUIZ

1. **No one wants to spend an entire weekend doing housework. What ideas can you generate to get some of the work done throughout the week so it doesn't become a huge chore?**

2. **Using the chart on the following page, list out what you can do each day (or even every other day) to keep your domicile picked up and clean. Think about picking up trash, emptying garbage cans, taking dishes to the kitchen and washing them, putting your clothes away, taking dirty clothes to the laundry room, and so forth. Really break it down.**

Housecleaning Chart

Notes					
Saturday					
Friday					
Thursday					
Wednesday					
Tuesday					
Monday					
Sunday					
	Pick Up House ☐ Straighten ☐ Put things away ☐ Take out garbage ☐ Take out recycling	**Clean Bathrooms** ☐ Wipe down toilet ☐ Clean toilet bowl ☐ Clean sink, wipe counter ☐ Wipe off mirror ☐ Wipe out tub/shower ☐ Sweep/mop floor	**Clean Kitchen** ☐ Empty/fill dishwasher ☐ Clean sink ☐ Wipe down counters ☐ Wipe down stovetop ☐ Wipe off kitchen table ☐ Sweep/mop floor	**Dust** ☐ Furniture ☐ Picture frames	**Vacuum** ☐ Carpets/rugs ☐ Sweep floors

Laundry Basics

I joke that one of the most important transitions to adulthood is pink underwear. At least once in nearly everyone's young life we make the mistake of putting whites with something red and then wash them together in hot water. The result? Pink underwear. You can dare to be different by reading this section, foregoing this life lesson.

How Often Do I Need to Wash Things?

Most clothes don't need to be washed every day unless you work in a really dirty job like as an automechanic or a garbage collector. For most office and retail jobs, less is fine for some articles of clothes.

- ❑ **Undershirts, underwear, socks and T-shirts** — once and only once. These are close to your body, and absorb sweat and oil. Make sure you have 10 of each to easily get through a week.

- ❑ **Jeans, khakis, and shorts** — 2 or 3 times. Most of us will spill something on our pants, or rub up against a dirty car, or just accumulate grime in 2-3 days.

- ❑ **Button-down shirts and sweaters** — 1-2 times, depending on how much you sweat or how dirty you got. When in doubt, wash it.

- ❑ **Pajamas** — This depends on your age, how much you sweat, and frankly if you are sleeping with someone else, but typically, 2-3 nights max.

- ❑ **Towels** — once a week.

- ❑ **Bed sheets** — every 1 or 2 weeks, especially if you have allergies or have acne -- get that bacteria and grime away from your skin!

Separate Your Clothes

This, my friends, is the key to laundry. Dump all of your clothes on the floor, and make piles thusly. Follow the instructions in the chart on how to wash these items.

Laundry Items	Washer Settings	Detergent, Etc.	Notes
Whites, lightweight fabrics (socks, underwear, T-shirts, button down shirts)	Hot water, regular cycle	1 scoop detergent, 1 small scoop brightener, fabric softener	Dry on hot, take out button down shirts while still a bit damp, and hang them on hangers,
Coloreds, lightweight and knits (socks, underwear, T-shirts, light button-down shirts)	Cold water, regular cycle	1 scoop detergent, 1 small scoop brightener, fabric softener	Dry on warm-hot, take out button down shirts while still damp, and hang on hangers.
Jeans and other heavy dark items (NOT towels)	Warm water, regular cycle	1 scoop detergent, fabric softener	Dry on hot.
White towels and sheets	Hot water, regular cycle	1 scoop detergent, 1 small scoop brightener, fabric softener	Dry on hot.
Colored towels and sheets	Warm water, regular cycle	1 scoop detergent, fabric softener	Dry on warm-hot.

IMPORTANT NOTE: Don't cram too much stuff into the wash – do two loads. Clothes should be loosely placed in the washer, and come up no further than 3/4 of the way to the top. Otherwise, your clothes don't get clean and your washer may break down from abuse.

Reading Laundry Labels

It's a good idea to read the laundry labels in your clothes to determine how best to wash them. Read through the graphics below for information on what those wacky symbols mean.

Washing

	Cotton Wash (no bar underneath image) Maximum wash – the number within the washtub is the maximum wash temperature		**Any bleach allowed** Chlorine based bleaching allowed, only cold and dilute solution
	Synthetics Wash / mild treatment (single bar) Medium wash (mild washing conditions).		**Only oxygen bleach/non-chlorine bleach allowed**
	Wool Wash / very mild treatment (double bar) Minimum wash (delicate washing conditions)		**Do not bleach**
	Hand Wash Only Do not machine wash. Wash by hand, maximum temperature 40°C, handle with care.		**May be dry cleaned**
	Not suitable for washing		**May be dry cleaned** (this letter tells the dry cleaner what process is required)
			Do not dry clean or remove stains with solvents

Drying

	May be tumble dried		**Dry flat** Recommended for garments which are easily distorted by vertical drying.
	Tumble dry low (low heat setting)		**Hang / Line dry** For garments not distorted by vertical drying or where tumble drying is not recommended.
	Tumble dry high (high heat setting)		**Drip dry** Recommended for garments which will withstand distortion and are generally synthetic in nature.
	Do not tumble dry		

Ironing

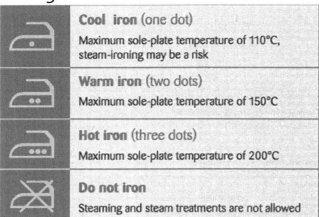

	Cool iron (one dot) Maximum sole-plate temperature of 110°C, steam-ironing may be a risk
	Warm iron (two dots) Maximum sole-plate temperature of 150°C
	Hot iron (three dots) Maximum sole-plate temperature of 200°C
	Do not iron Steaming and steam treatments are not allowed

Washing Large Items (Blankets, Sleeping Bags, etc.)

Some items don't easily fit into a standard washer, and thus may not get clean. Take these types of items to your neighborhood Laundromat or take them into a dry cleaner who does laundry.

Stain Removal Chart

Yep, we all get into grime. This chart will help you figure out how to degrime your clothing.

Stain	Solvent	Method	Notes
Oil, grease, tar, asphalt, gum, fresh paint, ballpoint ink & related stains	Use a 'volatile dry solvent' (like 70-90% isopropyl rubbing alcohol, K2R spotter, paint thinner, etc.)	Agitate (tamp, rub gently, or distribute chemical evenly), then blot. Continue blotting until the stain no longer transfers to your cloth, or until the stain disappears.	Rinse with warm water or flush with a personal extractor (such as a carpet cleaning machine with water-only rinse setting).
Dry paint, lacquer, varnish, nail polish, shoe polish, lipstick, magic marker & related stains	Use paint, oil, and grease remover (paint or lacquer thinner; clear, non-acetone fingernail polish remover, etc. Caution, can dissolve carpet latex.)	Agitate (tamp, rub gently, or distribute chemical evenly), then blot. Continue blotting until the stain no longer transfers to your cloth, or until the stain disappears.	Rinse with warm water or flush with a personal extractor (such as a carpet cleaning machine with water-only rinse setting).
Fruit punch, red wine, grape juice, decaf coffee, mustard & related stains	Use a general purpose spotter - includes most general spotters available at the grocer or carpet retailer.	Agitate (tamp, rub gently, or distribute chemical evenly), then blot. Continue blotting until the stain no longer transfers to your cloth, or until the stain disappears.	Rinse with warm water or flush with a personal extractor (such as a carpet cleaning machine with water-only rinse setting).
Pigment, copier toner, graphite & related stains	Use a general purpose spotter - includes most general spotters available at the grocer or carpet retailer.	Agitate (tamp, rub gently, or distribute chemical evenly), then blot. Continue blotting until the stain no longer transfers to your cloth, or until the stain disappears.	Rinse with warm water or flush with a personal extractor (such as a carpet cleaning machine with water-only rinse setting).
Protein: egg, milk, blood, urine stain & related stains	Scoop up and/or blot excess. Use an oxygen bleach (hydrogen peroxide based) stain remover. If needed, reapply cleaning chemical evenly, agitate, then blot again until the stain no longer transfers to your cloth or the stain disappears.	Agitate (tamp, rub gently, or distribute chemical evenly), then blot. Continue blotting until the stain no longer transfers to your cloth, or until the stain disappears.	Rinse with warm water or flush with a personal extractor (such as a carpet cleaning machine with water-only rinse setting).
General soil, food spots, ketchup, candy, coffee, tea, cola spills & related stains	Scoop up and/or blot excess. Use an oxygen bleach (hydrogen peroxide based) stain remover.	Agitate (tamp, rub gently, or distribute chemical evenly), then blot. Continue blotting until the stain no longer transfers to your cloth, or until the stain disappears.	Rinse with warm water or flush with a personal extractor (such as a carpet cleaning machine with water-only rinse setting).

Mending Basics

Keeping clothes in good repair isn't hard, and it's a whole lot cheaper than buying new clothes just because you have a rip or a missing button. This section contains information on sewing basics that everyone should know.

Iron-on Patches

1. One of the greatest inventions of our time is the iron-on patch. Use these for larger tears or for places that get a lot of wear, such as knees, and where pockets attach to pants.

2. Select a patch that closely matches the fabric you are repairing.

3. Cut a piece of patch that is slightly larger than the tear. If possible, round the edges so that they don't pull off the clothing.

4. Set your iron to the recommended setting for the fabric you are repairing and wait until it is hot.

5. Turn the article of clothing inside out.

6. Place the patch shiny-side down over the tear.

7. Iron the patch into place by slowing moving the iron in small circles over the entire patch, paying particular attention to the edges and corners. Continue for 30 seconds.

8. Lift the iron and let cool.

9. Check the patch. If not securely adhered, repeat steps 6 and 7.

How to Sew on a Button

Buttons come off, and it's easy to sew them back on if you know how to do it.

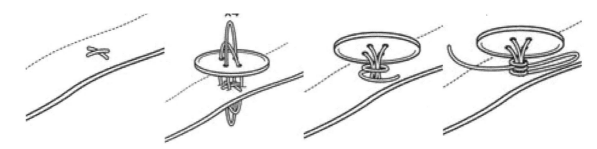

1. **Start with twelve inches of thread,** knotted securely at one end, and thread your needle. Make a single stitch in the shirt in line with the row of buttons, about 1/8 inch long, and then make another stitch perpendicular to the first.

2. **Hold the button** about 1/8 inch away from the shirt and thread the needle up through one hole in the button and down the diagonally opposite hole. Do the same with the other holes and then repeat four times.

3. **Wrap the thread** tightly around the 1/8 inch shank that has been created between the button and the cloth to create a tight loop of thread.

4. **Push the needle through** this loop a few times and cut the thread close to it.

EXERCISE 12— CLOTHING CARE ACTIVITY

You've had some exposure to how to care for clothing now. While no one expects you to be an expert, you can refer to this information in the future. In the meantime, here are a couple of exercises:

1. Our first activity is to try your hand at sewing on a button. The instructor will hand out needles, thread, buttons, and scraps of cloth.

2. Next, take a look at the laundry labels in your jacket or hoodie, or take a peek at the label in another student's collar. Ask permission first! How would you wash this garment?

3. Finally, the t-shirt folding contest! Break into two groups, and hand out an even number of t-shirts. At the word Go, each team should agree on the proper way to fold the t-shirts, and then fold them all the same way. The team that finishes first, with a stack of neatly folded T-shirts, wins. No fair having one person do the work! Everyone needs to pitch in!

SECTION 3

HAVING FUN

Let's Have Fun!

This section is all about fun, how to have it, how to plan for it, how to make it, and where to find it. Part of being an adult is learning how to have fun in your own way. That's right – when you are on your own, there may not be anyone there encouraging you to get out and have fun, or a sibling who is a built-in buddy. You have to do it all on your own.

Fun is something we absolutely need. It is a necessity. Without fun and joy in our lives, there really isn't much point, now is there? We each have fun in different ways, and that's fine. It doesn't matter if our idea of fun is doing crafting at home, or playing Settlers of Catan, or hang gliding off of a cliff in Mexico. What does matter is that we find enjoyment in our lives, no matter how we define it.

One thing to note: many people who are taking this class have a tendency to isolate – meaning, rather than seeking out others to be with, they tend to stay by themselves. Sometimes this is okay. Sometimes. However, we humans are social animals and we do need to be with other people, to interact with them, hang out with them, talk to them, and so on. So, part of this lesson means looking at ways that you can get out in the world a bit more.

Sound scary? It doesn't have to be. But like anything, it does take a little planning and a little work.

What Are Friendships?

Friendships are relationships we build over time, typically based on shared values, interests, and to some degree, location.

Our friendships typically form in places like schools, churches, work, clubs, and neighborhoods with people we enjoy being with. We feel safe with our friends, and enjoy doing activities with them. Sometimes, the best friends are those with whom you can do nothing, and still be comfortable!

We tend to make friends at specific junctures in our lives: in elementary school, in middle and high school, and potentially in college and at work. However, as we get older, many of us find that we have to work a bit harder to develop friendships. If we have children, we may prefer to hang out with other parents, or with people who have no children if we are childless. We might want to associate with people who like to travel the world, or people who like to game online. While we may keep our older relationships from when we were younger, many people find that they wish to have friendships with people who have similar interests, and interests may change over time.

So that's what friendships are – but how are they formed? According to research, friendships require:

- ❏ **Repeated & Unplanned Interactions:** This means being at the same place, at the same time, over and over again, with the same person or people. This allows two strangers to interact, find out if they have anything in common, and if so, to develop a friendship over time. For this reason, schools, work, clubs and online gaming rooms are popular ways to meet people.

- ❏ **Proximity:** Being physically close enough to other people to actually interact with them is important for developing friendships. You might see someone on the train tracks going the opposite direction every day, but if you're not close enough to strike up a conversation, you're going to lose out. Online chat and gaming rooms are good ways to converse with others and find out if you have any affinity. The downside is, you may not live close to the people you associate with. This doesn't mean that people you meet online are not your friends, but everyone also needs friends in real life – people you can go have pizza with, who can take you to the doctor if you sprain your ankle, someone to wait with in line to see the next DC movie!

- ❏ **A Setting That Encourages Vulnerability:** No, this doesn't mean that you need to be in a padded room with a box of tissues, but it does mean that wherever you meet, you are able in some part to be your genuine self. For example, if you go to church because your family insists, but you really are not a believer and rather hate it, striking up friendships there with deeply religious peers may not work well as you may not have enough shared values with them. No one wants to be in a relationship—especially a friendship—where you have to pretend to be someone you are not.

EXERCISE 1 — DESCRIBE FRIENDSHIPS

List five things that you think describe friendships:

1.

2.

3.

4.

5.

Steps You Can Take to Make Friends

Here are some ideas to get you started making new friends around your area:

- ❏ **Try to chat up your neighbors.** You may have lots in common with the people who live near you, such as in your apartment building or neighborhood. You might see someone each morning at Starbucks who is on a gaming server that you are familiar with—ask about it! Be alert to the people around you. You might discover a friendship just waiting to bloom!

- ❏ **Reconnect with old friends and acquaintances.** Whether from high school or college or previous jobs, you may want to reach out to people you connected with at other times in your life. They may be looking to broaden their social networks, too, and if you had things in common once, you very well may have things in common now.

- ❏ **If you're religious or spiritual, connect with a church, synagogue, yoga center etc.** Local religious organizations are one of the most sure-fire ways to meet new people and make new friends. You automatically find folks who are likely to have similar values as you.

- ❏ **Make actual plans.** Most of us will say something like "Let's get together sometime," and then never follow up. Don't be one of those people! See if you can get something concrete on the calendar right away: "What are you doing in two weeks? Would you like to go see the new Star Wars movie?" You don't want to be pushy, but you do want to be concrete.

❑ **Have a hobby and be open to meeting people while doing it.** Many of our clients have a favorite "special interest" which could include things like Magic the Gathering or Dungeons and Dragons (yes, really, even adults play these games), poker, crafting, building computers, writing fan fiction. You name it, there is almost certainly someone else out there who has the same interest. You just need to be active in your interests, and then find others active in the same, or similar, activities.

❑ **Take advantage of the internet.** Sites like Meetup.com make it very easy to find groups around you that have similar interests. It's also no pressure. You can scan events happening in your area, and decide whether or not to go – no one is keeping an attendance sheet. Though once you do RSVP for an event, actually go!

❑ **Connect with your coworkers.** This one can be a bit tricky. Coworker relationships are often complex – you never really know where work/career aspirations end and true friendship begins. You have to test the waters and perhaps attend a few networking events together or a happy hour after work. Be open to this, but also don't feel bad about maintaining barriers between work and play if that is more comfortable for you.

❑ **Open your house for meals and get-togethers.** Once you have met a few people that you'd like to get to know better (from work, from the neighborhood, from a Meetup group) you can host a small get together at your home. This could be to game, to watch a movie, to do a crafting project, or to just hang out. We'll talk more about how to have a get-together later in this section.

EXERCISE 2 — WHAT MAKES YOU A GOOD FRIEND?

List five things about yourself that make you an interesting friend:

1.

2.

3.

4.

5.

Now, list three things you are willing to try to make yourself an even better friend:

1.

2.

3.

Having a Great Social Life

One of the best ways to have a great (or even better) social life is to meet more people and do more things. Sadly, interesting people who want to be friends don't magically show up at our door. We have to go out into the real world to find them. And, we have to be interesting people ourselves in order to have friendships with other interesting people. It really is not that hard once you get the hang of it.

Exercise & Sports

One of the best ways to have fun – and to take care of our bodies and minds – is to either participate in a sport or to exercise. Many sports are group activities, and even if you don't play a particular sport, it's never too late to learn. Such sports include:

❑ Basketball

❑ Volleyball

❑ Bowling

❑ Tennis

❑ Golf

❑ Badminton

❑ Rock climbing

❑ Surfing

❑ Bicycling

❑ Running/jogging

❑ Hiking

❑ SCUBA diving

❑ Kayaking

If you live nearby or in a metropolitan area, you can find a club or organization for almost all of these sports nearby. Check online, check local community colleges, the YMCA, community centers, and local gyms and sports centers for more information.

Classes – For Fun!

The idea of going to school for fun may seem strange and bizarre, but many community, state, and private colleges offer classes for 'non-students' – those who are not enrolled and working toward earning a degree. And if you are enrolled for academics, you can still take classes for fun, just take them Pass/Not Pass. Additionally, private and public organizations in your area may offer classes as well. The variety of classes offered can be staggering:

- ❏ Wine/beer/food tasting
- ❏ Art/drawing
- ❏ Graphic design
- ❏ Foreign languages (Spanish, French, Japanese, etc)
- ❏ Dance (jazz, swing, hip hop, ballroom, etc.)

- ❏ Fencing
- ❏ Martial arts
- ❏ Yoga
- ❏ Swimming
- ❏ Cooking
- ❏ Music (guitar, piano, singing, etc.)

Getting Out

Okay, so maybe meeting once or twice a month with a group isn't enough fun, and maybe you'd like to meet some people who have different interests than yours – fair enough. But don't shut off the laptop yet. There are other groups of people you can easily meet and connect with. Here is just a partial list of the services that are available online to help you meet new folks in the area.

- ❏ **Meetup.com** – We talked about this earlier in the chapter, but it bears repeating. This is an online board where people can both create and join groups around a given interest. Whether its Corgi owners meeting each other and their dogs, or folks practicing yoga, you'll find all sorts of folks doing all sorts of things. Just go to the website, enter your zip code, and submit to find what all is happening around you. This is by far the biggest, and best, way to meet people socially.

- ❏ **Discord** – Yes, the same group that allows you to gang up on bosses in MMOs is also used in some areas as a way to get together for gaming IRL. Discord is frequently used by people playing Pokemon Go and LARP groups such as Vampires. You can also find information on Facebook and other social media.

- ❏ **Volunteermatch.org** – This online board is also a great way to get out and meet people while you're helping others. You can volunteer for a day at a time (river and beach clean up days) or for extended periods (animal rescue worker).

1. **Take a few minutes now to go over the ideas that have been presented so far, and list five things that you are willing to try in the next three months.**

   ❑ _____

   ❑ _____

   ❑ _____

   ❑ _____

   ❑ _____

2. **Look online and see where you might take a class, go to a group, or participate in a new activity. List them here:**

3. **Track your progress on your calendar by marking a reminder in one month to see if you are getting out and participating in new activities on a regular basis. Put a reminder on your calendar now!**

Social Etiquette

While we're talking about going out and trying new things, let's also review the basics of social interaction. For better or for worse, social etiquette – also called manners – matters. Really. Behaving in socially-acceptable ways, for the most part, anyway, really does make life run more smoothly. If you remember that the vast majority of social etiquette is based on the Golden Rule ("Do unto others as you would have others do unto you"), you can understand why this is true.

❑ **Courtesy and Respect.** All people deserve to be treated with courtesy and respect. This means that saying *please* and *thank you,* holding doors open for other people behind you, offering your seat to someone else, giving your full attention to someone who is speaking to you (put down the book, phone, or laptop) are still important aspects of civility regardless of your age and gender. Remember that no one owes you respect unless you are willing to give it in return. This applies to potential friends, potential employers, and potential dating partners! If you want people to like and respect you, you must treat them with courtesy and respect.

- **Conversations.** Don't dominate a conversation. Don't interrupt or talk over people. Don't dismiss other people's opinions. Let other people talk and express their opinions, too. It's okay to have a heated debate and be passionate about what you are discussing, but name-calling and swearing are completely off limits. If you inadvertently offend someone or make a mistake, apologize as soon as possible. If you have the opposite challenge, and don't speak up at all, make sure to look interested in the conversation, rather than staring at a wall or your cell phone. If you look interested in what is being said, someone might just ask you a direct question, and then you're in!

- **Promptness.** Be on time. If you have an appointment at 2 pm, then you need to be there at 2 pm. Not 2:15 or 2:05. Being late essentially tells the other person that his/her time is not as important as yours, which is extremely rude. And, if someone asks you a question, or sends you an invitation, you owe them a prompt answer. If you don't have the information yet, or you're not sure you can make it to an event, let the person know that, and then get back to them as soon as you can with a more definitive answer. Don't leave people hanging!

- **Gratitude.** Show it. Mean it. When someone does something nice for you, even if it is to say thank you to you, don't let it go unanswered. There is far too little human kindness and gratitude for what we each have, and it makes the world a colder place. No one owes you anything, really. Acknowledge and show gratitude for whatever you have and what people do for you, even small gestures.

- **Table Manners.** When you're eating alone at home, no one cares if you slurp your soup, wipe your hands on your clothes, or have food hanging off your face. However, if you are eating with other people or are out in public, you owe it to other diners not to gross them out in these ways. Chew with your mouth closed, don't stuff food in your mouth, don't talk with food in your mouth, and keep the belching to yourself and excuse yourself! If you find yourself in more formal settings. Watch how others are behaving and model their behavior if there is any doubt how you should be comporting yourself. This trick can be a lifesaver if you don't know which fork to use, how to get a roll from the other side of the table, or what to do with the finger towel someone gave you!

- **Public Behavior.** Like with your eating habits, your general demeanor in the privacy of your own home may well be different than your behavior in the world beyond, and that's fine. But, do remember that people with dirty clothes, untied shoes, dirty hair and stinky bodies are not socially acceptable except in a barnyard. And if you're acting like a jerk in public by swearing, yelling or making a scene, people will flee from you as if you were a crazy person. You don't have to be perfect, you just have to clean and appropriate.

EXERCISE 4— HOW ARE YOUR MANNERS?

1. What social etiquette skills are you really great at in public or in home?

2. What skills do you think you could work on?

3. What 'breach' of social etiquette (breaking a social rule) makes you crazy?

Now, partner up!

1. Ask your partner what you think his/her best social etiquette skill is, and write it down.

2. Next, tell each other what skill you want to work on and how you think you can work on it. Write down here what your partner thinks you need to work on:

Personal Space

Everyone needs personal space, and some of us need more than others. Typically, personal space is the invisible boundary we have around us that if encroached upon, we feel invaded and uncomfortable. How much distance is comfortable depends on:

- ❑ **How well you know the person.** Getting a hug or a peck on the cheek might be fine from your mom, but not so fine from a stranger!

- ❑ **What the situation is.** If you are meeting someone for the first time and they offer to shake your hand, that's socially acceptable touch. Grabbing someone randomly, or insisting on holding that person's hand for a long period of time, not so much.

- ❑ **What the environment is.** Sometimes we are forced to be in close quarters with other people, such as in a theater, an elevator, or standing in line. Keep your hands to yourself, don't fling your backpack or purse around, don't sigh loudly or mumble to yourself. Be still, keep quiet, and then move on!

In terms of physical space, keep these guidelines in mind:

- ❑ 2 feet — friends and family
- ❑ 4 feet —acquaintances, co-workers, and 'superiors' like teachers and employers
- ❑ 6-8 feet — very senior staff (the CEO), celebrities, public officials

Body Language and Nonverbal Communication

Much of what we convey to other people is not based on what we say, but on how we say it, and what we do — also known as nonverbal communication. In fact, most experts agree that only around 10% of communication is the actual verbal message, and the rest of the communication is tone and body language.

Let's look at what our bodies are saying when we're with other people.

Head

- ❑ Head lowered might mean that the person is shy or afraid to speak.
- ❑ Genuine smiles can be detected by 'crinkling' of the eyes. A false smile usually only engages the lips.
- ❑ A titled head typically shows interest or concern.
- ❑ Nodding while listening means both engagement and agreement.

Upper Body

- ❑ Slouched shoulders can mean fatigue and depression. Standing erect signifies strength and forcefulness.
- ❑ Open arms means open communication, and closed arms typically mean closed down to communication.

Lower Body

- ❑ Hands on hips means readiness and eagerness. It can sometimes mean aggression, as well.
- ❑ Jiggling your leg or foot shows boredom or impatience.
- ❑ Crossing your legs away from someone shows disinterest, and crossing them toward someone shows interest.

Eyes

- ❑ Eye contact typically means that the listener and the speaker are engaged.
- ❑ Lowered eyes can mean fear or guilt.
- ❑ Squinting indicates an attempt to understand
- ❑ Eye contact typically signifies confidence and interest.
- ❑ Looking sideways or up quickly (rolling your eyes) signifies annoyance.
- ❑ When we are trying to think, we typically look straight up. If we are recalling an emotion, we typically look up and left, and if we are trying to recall a fact, we typically look up and to the right.

Openness vs. Defensiveness

Expectancy vs. Frustration

Evaluation vs. Suspicion

Self-control vs. Nervousness

Readiness vs. Boredom

Confidence vs. Insecurity

Pair up for this exercise. Take turns expressing these following scenarios, with one person acting out the emotion or expression, and the other person writing down what s/he is seeing in terms of body language that expresses this emotion or expression.

- ❏ Shame/humiliation
- ❏ Defensive
- ❏ Happy
- ❏ Nervous

- ❏ Anger/frustration
- ❏ Open and calm
- ❏ Eager
- ❏ Bored

Now, take turns expressing and documenting the following:

- ❏ Ready to talk and engage
- ❏ Disinterested in talking/engaging

Discuss your findings together! Write down below the areas that your partner thinks you might want to work on in the future:

Socializing and Making Small Talk

Many people struggle to socialize and make small talk, and yet these are often the beginnings of all social relationships, from friendships to life partners. Socializing beyond high school doesn't have to be terrifying or traumatizing. We'll go over some basics here, but do remember that practicing these skills whenever you can will help greatly.

The Do's:

- ❏ **Scan the room and find other people standing alone** – Pretty much at any social function there are people who also feel awkward and alone at social gatherings. Approach them, say hello and introduce yourself, and perhaps even comment on how hard it is to attend these sorts of functions. You may have just found an ally for the evening!

- ❏ **Initiate conversation** – Be the person who initiates conversation and breaks the ice is when you are out in public. You can comment on the weather ("This weather is gorgeous!"), on the long line you are waiting in ("I sure wish they'd hire more checkers"), on the dog the other person is walking ("That is a lovely dog, what breed is it?") and more. Don't get too personal ("Are you pregnant?"), don't get political ("You didn't really vote for Hillary, did you?") and don't get dark ("End of days, the world is coming to an end!"). Keep it light and cheerful, smile, and people will generally reciprocate.

- ❑ **Smile** – People who are smiling (not grinning like a fool – *smiling*) are more approachable. Happier people draw more happiness to themselves, so smile and lighten up.

- ❑ **Enjoy yourself** – When you look like you're having fun you are instantly more likable. If you're enjoying yourself, people will notice and want in on the action.

- ❑ **Acknowledge other people** – This can be as simple as a smile and a nod. When you make eye contact with a stranger, acknowledge it with a smile and a nod.

- ❑ **Listen** – Most everyone loves talking about themselves and their interests. But if you are the one doing all the talking, you're not having a conversation, you're talking at people. Take a genuine interest in people. Ask them questions and follow-up questions. Share your own views (within reason), but give the other person plenty of time to chat.

- ❑ **Keep eye contact** – Don't scan the room while talking to someone. It is a clear indication you're not interested in the conversation. If you really have no interest in what someone is saying, gently change the topic: "Hey! Did you happen to see the last episode of...?" Or excuse yourself and find another person to chat with: "Gosh, I promised my friend I'd try to find him here. It's been nice chatting with you!"

- ❑ **Keep open body language** – Whether alone or not, avoid closing yourself off by crossing your arms. Remain open, active, interested, and approachable.

The Don'ts:

- ❑ **Stare at your phone incessantly** – Most of us will nervously check our phone if feeling awkward in public, but it's a good idea to scan the room to see if anyone is looking at us in an effort to engage. And certainly, if someone is actually trying to talk to us, put the darn phone down!

- ❑ **Ignore other people** – As above, don't stare at your shoes, your phone, or the wall. Scan the room with a small smile on your face, look interested, and ready to engage.

- ❑ **Ask the same questions** – If you have already asked a person previously what s/he does for a living, try not to ask that question again. Instead, ask how his or her job is going, or how the person spent the weekend. Or, you can ask if the person has seen any movies or live music lately, and ask more about that.

- ❑ **Criticize** – It's OK to give your critique of the music or selection of beers, but don't go on a tirade. Try to find something upbeat to talk about instead.

Break up into groups of threes for this activity, and number yourselves 1, 2, and 3. Standing separately, person 2 should go up to person 1 and start a conversation, asking questions, responding, and taking turns in conversation. After a few turns, person 3 should walk up and join the conversation. Continue talking together as a group for a total of five minutes (timed). Then, answer these questions:

1. **What was hard about being person 2 and instigating a conversation?**

2. **What was hard about being person 3 and joining the conversation?**

3. **What would have made this easier or harder? What worked and what didn't work?**

4. **What might you try next time you start or join a conversation**

Dating and Romance

You'll note that this section comes after discussions about socializing and making friends. That's because those are important first steps to take before you begin dating. Dating depends on reasonable social skills – the ability to talk to people, do things with them comfortably, and occasionally communicate about difficult topics. You must be able to do these things before dating. So if you're rough, work on those skills first!

Dating Basics

Ah, dating. One of the most sucky things people do in life. There's nothing quite like setting yourself up for rejection after rejection to build your confidence, eh? The important thing to know at the outset is: it happens to all of us. We all get rejected, we all get our hearts broken. It's the human condition.

One of the most important things to remember is that *you* are *also* going to be doing some rejecting as well. Whether you are looking at online profiles or going to functions in person, you are also sifting through the faces and profiles and deciding who you might be interested in, and who you are not interested in. So, don't take the rejection thing too hard, because we all go through it and *we all do it*.

Here are some tips before we get started:

- ❏ **A '7' attracts a '7'** – This is a hard one for many people to understand, but really attractive people are typically attracted to *other* really attractive people, for better or for worse. You will always have better luck dating other people who are about as attractive, inside *and* out, as you. You can certainly up your game a bit by improving your personal appearance, your wardrobe, and your body language. You can also improve your self-confidence and how interesting you are by getting out and doing more. But also remember that massively attractive people may look good, but can be hopelessly boring and self-centered.

- ❏ **It begins with you** – As above, make sure you are putting forth real effort in improving yourself as a potential mate. This doesn't mean that you have to become someone else or be a fake, but it does mean that if you want to date someone who looks good, you also need to look good. If you want someone who is interesting to talk with, then you should also be interesting to talk with. If you want to date someone who has money, you need to earn money. Develop yourself!

- ❏ **People are different** – It's important to realize that everyone is different, and may have differing opinions, ways of conducting their lives, and interests. The best way to get to know people (and for them to feel comfortable around you) is to find out more about the people you are dating, and to not be judgmental about their likes and dislikes. There are many ways of being in the world, and yours is only one.

- ❏ **Gendered Males and Females are often different** – In non-obvious ways! Biological guys tend to want more freedom and space than women, who often like to spend more time just being together. Men may want to be more spur of the moment, and women may want to know when they will be seeing a new partner next. Men often have a 'grosser' sense of humor and romance than women appreciate. Of course this is all very generalized, and gender expression itself is highly variable. By and large however, dating partners, at least at first, often appreciate being treated more carefully than you would treat a very close friend until you understand what makes them comfortable.

- **Dating is confusing** – Sometimes when you are dating someone, that person starts acting strangely. Either the person may call all the time or just disappear for a few days. Try not to sweat it. We all have good days and bad days, days when we feel like chatting and days we don't. Try not to read too much into it, but pay attention to it. Is the person just having a bad day or week? Or is the person becoming too dependent or actually ignoring you? Talk to a trusted friend if you are concerned. And remember: no one likes a stalker. If someone doesn't respond to you, incessant texting isn't going to make that person more eager to talk. It's a turn off!

- **Be honest** – Are you looking to make friends? Find a monogamous partner? Casually date? Do you not know? All of this is OK. What's important for you and what's important for the people you meet is that you be as honest as possible. This will prevent a lot of drama for both sides. Most people will respect you for being true to your own feeling and what you're ready for, rather than telling them what they want to hear, and potentially dealing with a lot of hurt feelings all around. Don't get me wrong, don't be a jerk about it. If someone says that they want to be exclusive with you and you're not interested you can say, "Thank you, but I'm just not interested in a committed relationship right now." Do not string the person along hoping that s/he will be satisfied with a 'friends with benefits' arrangement. It's destructive and toxic unless you are certain the other person also wants a 'physical only' relationship.

EXERCISE 7— DATING!

1. Do you think you have realistic expectations about who you would like to date? Why or why not?

2. What qualities are you attracted to in a dating partner?

3. What are the advantages and disadvantages of being up front about what you're looking for in a dating partner?

4. Can you think of ways to be honest without hurting the other person?

How to Meet People to Date

Much like finding new friends, there are essentially four ways to meet people to date:

1. **By complete chance** – for example, bumping into someone at the supermarket.

2. **By getting set up** – where someone you know sets you up with someone s/he thinks you'll like.

3. **By participating in an activity that you both like** – for example, by taking a class, joining a cooking club, going to church, volunteering for a political cause, or going hiking with a group of people on Sundays.

4. **By actively searching for someone to date** – for example, by joining Match.com, eHarmony, okcupid, or one of the several dating services/sites.

Of the above methods, number one will pretty much ensure that you spend your life alone. Method number two might work, but the chances are pretty slim unless you know a lot of people who know a lot of other people who are 'in the market'.

That leaves options three and four, which really are the best ways to meet people if you are serious about finding a romantic partner. The reason is this: when you meet people randomly, you might be physically attracted to them, but there is no way to know that they are a) single, b) interested in dating you, or c) have anything in common with you at all.

When you meet people through a social group surrounding an activity (like an anime club) you know that you have at least one thing in common with that person, and potentially much more. When you meet people through a dating service, you know that they are interested in dating. When you participate in a dating group that hosts activities that you like, you know that you have in something in common with these people AND that they are interested in dating. This obviously increases your odds.

So, spend a little time searching around the internet for likely sites. For activities, again, check out Meetup.com (which may have nothing to do with dating, be forewarned). If you're interested in checking out the autism dating scene, you can search the internet for 'autism dating' or 'neurodiverse dating' – there are new sites coming up all the time.

Asking Someone Out

Let's say you've done your homework and found a great social group to join, and you've attended a couple of activities. There's a cute someone who smiles at you once in a while, and you've chatted with her/him once or twice. You like the person, it seems like s/he likes you too. Maybe the person has paid you special attention to you a few times and you're ready for the next step.

- ❑ Invite the special individual to join you for a coffee drink after the event (if you can).
- ❑ Invite the special individual for a coffee drink sometime next week.

The point is to start off small. You don't want to overwhelm the other person and you don't want to overwhelm yourself. This is why we are so often instructed to "play it casual" when we first meet someone. It can be an overwhelming and anxiety-inducing experience to try to create a relationship and build rapport with someone you've just met.

Pay close attention to the reactions when you ask one of these questions – does the person smile? Pretty much, the bigger the smile, the bigger the YES! So even if the person says s/he can't make it, the smile is probably telling you that s/he would if s/he could – so ask if another time would work. If you get a yes, give the person *your* phone number (or ask if you can text it to him or her), and tell the person that you hope to hear from him or her soon. If you ask someone out and s/he's not available for that specific time/date, it is then that person's turn to respond with "But I'm free next Thursday." You can keep this type of response in mind if you are invited to spend time with someone, and you're interested but not available – make sure you respond with when you *would* be free to see him/her so that there isn't confusion.

If s/he doesn't smile, then the answer will probably be no. That's okay. Take a deep breath, and keep going to the events. There may be someone else who turns up who you might be interested in, so don't give up!

IMPORTANT NOTE: Some people are not as expressive with their face as others. In this case, if you get turned down when you ask, "Would you like to join me at Starbucks after the hike (or whatever the group activity is)," you should always follow up with "Another time, maybe? I'll give you my number." That way, it is up to the other person to call, and if s/he is interested, s/he will probably call.

At the End of Your First Date

At the end of your first date, you need to decide if you want to see this person again. Did it go well? Were you fairly comfortable with the other person? Did you have things in common? If so, ask if you can call him/her again. If the answer is yes, make sure you get a phone number, and then call or text – preferably within a few days. If you call or text too quickly, the other person might feel pressured. If you wait too long, s/he may think you are not interested! Suggest a time and activity for a second meeting, and go from there!

The Importance of Hygiene in Social Interactions

When you are clean – and you smell clean – other people find it easier to be close to you. When you take care of your hygiene needs every day, it is easier to think well of yourself, and others will think more highly of you as well.

Straight up, it's just not sexy to go on a date without first sprucing up a bit. If you haven't showered, shaved, combed your hair, brushed your teeth, and put on a set of clean clothes from head to toe, chances are your date just may choose to stay clear of you and not give you a second (or third, or fourth) chance. And note: wearing perfume or cologne instead of showering and wearing clean clothes does not cut it. Remember, you may not be able to smell your own body odor, but others can, even through fragrance.

So if you're hoping for a hello hug or a goodnight squeeze from that great date and you'd like to get to date two, fresh and clean is sexy and definitely "in" —and will never go out of style.

Hygiene Hazards

- ❑ Greasy/unbrushed hair (wash and brush your hair)
- ❑ Body odor (shower with soap and use deodorant)
- ❑ Bad breath (brush, floss, and use mouthwash)
- ❑ Too much cologne or perfume (use very little if any at all)
- ❑ Unshaven, unruly everything (well kept facial 'scruff' is okay, but wild and woolly is not)
- ❑ Dirty hands or dirt lodged under the fingernails (scrub those hands)
- ❑ Boogers dangling (use a tissue!)
- ❑ Torn or stained clothes (wear your best, clean, casual clothes)

1. **Why do you think it's important to practice good hygiene when dating (if not at other times)?**

2. **What reaction might you have if your date showed up with dirty hair and clothes?**

3. **What two things can you start doing to improve your 'datability' in this area?**

Flirting and the First Kiss

So, you've seen a certain someone special once or twice, and you seem to like each other. You smile at each other, laugh at each other's jokes, and maybe even held hands. You might give each other little sideways glances, you might get a little tongue-tied, and giggle a lot. You're flirting!

If you've gotten this far with someone, then a first kiss probably isn't too far off. Finding the perfect moment for that kiss is a matter of timing, opportunity, and well, magic. For a first kiss, it's always a good idea to ask — May I kiss you? If you've been out more than two or three times, the chances are very good s/he'll say yes. Lean in and go for it. Short and sweet to start, and over time, you can work up to more. Go slow!

The 'I Love You' Moment

If things are progressing along for a while, you may start feeling like you never want to be apart from this person. You may think about him or her all the time, about doing special things for this person, and so on. Could you be falling in love? You might be.

But before you go too crazy, be a little careful about 'spilling the beans' and telling your friend that you love him/her. Some people get nervous when they are told someone is in love with them. So, again, go slow. Watch for signs that the other person might feel the same way, but remember, there is no rush.

Sex

If you are reading this section before you have read the previous sections, stop now, and go back and read those first. You absolutely need to learn the basics of friendship and dating before you are anywhere near ready for this step.

Readiness

Okay, now that you've read the other sections, and practiced all of the skills we discussed, we can begin the conversation about sex.

The first question you must answer is if you and your partner are actually ready to take this step. One of the ways to know if you are ready is if you can talk about whether you are both ready. If you can't talk about it, then you are probably not ready.

Before the chance for sex even occurs, you need to ensure that:

- ❑ You are both ready to have sex together
- ❑ You have protection against unwanted pregnancy and/or sexually-transmitted diseases
- ❑ You both realize that no method of protection may be 100% guaranteed
- ❑ You both understand the magnitude of this, to be taken with mutual respect for the other person. This is a big deal.

If you are uncomfortable about talking to your doctor about sex, then look up the closest Planned Parenthood location, and set up a counseling appointment. You need to talk to a health professional about both preventing pregnancy and about safer sex practices.

Next, remember that having sex is a big decision. If you are not ready, don't feel pressured to have sex just 'because everyone does it'. First off, not everyone does have sex before marriage and secondly, it's always your choice – and the choice of the other person.

Consent

And, speaking of choice: it is important to always make sure, by asking, if the other person wants to have sex. If you hear anything but Yes, you must stop.

No one has the right – EVER – to force sex on another person. Even if you are hot and heavy with someone and you are completely naked and ready to go, if the other person says STOP, you MUST STOP. The reverse is true as well. No matter how far you have gone, you can always stop. No one has the right to coerce you or force you to have sex. That is rape, pure and simple. Let's spell out what rape really looks like:

- ❑ If someone says No, it means no. STOP.
- ❑ If you try to coerce the person into having sex ("But you promised," "It will be okay," "I'll tell people we did it anyway,") you are behaving like a child. STOP.
- ❑ Anyone who is drunk or intoxicated, emotionally out of control, or incapacitated (not conscious) is not capable of giving consent, and you must STOP. Even if they said yes before, they cannot say yes now, so STOP.

Sex is always about respecting the other person's wishes as well as acting on your own. If there is any disconnect between what you want and what the other person wants, STOP.

EXERCISE 9— CONSENT

List three ways you know you do not have consent to have sex with another person:

1.

2.

3.

Other Things to Consider (Before Having Sex)

Before you take the big step, remember that sometimes sex between people changes things. To some, having sex may mean the expectation of 100% commitment as a couple. To others, it may mean expecting sex each time they see each other. Other people might expect having sex to be a one-time thing.

None of these are inherently wrong or bad, but if one person has expectations that are different than the other, you can see how this can cause problems. The best time to have these discussions is before you have sex. Things might change, and you may need to have this discussion again. Maybe you have been casually seeing someone and now you want to be exclusive. Maybe you have been exclusive and it is feeling too constraining. Things change. The most important thing is communication.

If you are confused about how you're feeling or what is happening with you and the partner, it is OK to bring up your concerns. If you've had sex with someone and don't want to do it again, or not at a given time, you are under no obligation. It is important to listen to your gut and be honest about your intentions. Anyone who is not willing to discuss these things, or dismisses your feelings as silly or immature, are not really ready for a relationship! You always have the right to feel as you do and to voice your concerns, and if anyone ever shuts you down, it's time to end the relationship. Intimacy of any sort without open and honest communication is degrading and dehumanizing. We are all worth more than that.

Finally, and most importantly, always be kind, gentle, and respectful. Sex is wonderful when you are with the right person, so be good to one another.

Sexual Health

Everyone needs to be concerned with their sexual health, even if they are not sexually active. If you don't feel comfortable having these conversations with your primary care physician, you can ask to see a specialist or you can go to your nearest Planned Parenthood for care.

Here are some general guidelines to follow, but work closely with your own doctor to make sure you are getting the care you need:

- ❑ **Women (including genetically female individuals who identify as male)**: All genetically female individuals should see a doctor as advised for PAP smears and breast exams.
- ❑ **Teen Boys and Girls**: The CDC now recommends that all men and women receive the HPV (Human Papillomavirus) vaccine, preferably before first sexual intercourse.
- ❑ **Young Adult Men and Women:** Although most people have been inoculated as children against Hepatitis A and B, check with your doctor to make sure.

- ❏ **Sexually Active Men and Women:** If you are having sex with multiple partners, even if protected, it is wise to have routine screenings for sexually-transmitted diseases. Some STDs can be present for quite some time without the person having any discomfort or symptoms, and early detection and treatment is vital not only for your own health, but also to protect your partners.

- ❏ **Everyone:** If you are experiencing pain, unusual discharges, or see visible lesions, bumps, or swelling on or near your genitals, refrain from sexual contact and see a doctor immediately.

Pregnancy and Sexually-Transmitted Disease Control

All sexually-active partners should be concerned about sexually-transmitted diseases (STDs) regardless of orientation or gender. Exchanging bodily fluids in any way can leave you at risk for infection. For heterosexual partners, an additional frequent concern is avoiding unwanted pregnancy. Some people prefer to use 'one time only' methods, and others (particularly those in committed, long-term relationships) prefer using more long-lasting methods. Both are described in the table below. Speak to your care provider about what method(s) are best for you and your partner. Do remember that NO method provides 100% protection from either pregnancy or disease transmittal.

Method	Pregnancy Protection	STD Protection
Condoms, Male	85-95% effective	Effective
Condoms, Female	85-95% effective	Effective
Vaginal Ring w/Spermacide	84-94% effective	Somewhat effective
Diaphragm w/Speramcide	84-94% effective	Somewhat effective
Progestin Injections/Implants	99% effective	Not effective
The Patch	99% effective	Not effective
Birth Control Pills	97-98% effective	Not effective

EXERCISE 10 — SEXUAL HEALTH

1. **What is the most effective way to avoid pregnancy during intercourse?**

2. **What is the most effective way to avoid STDs during intercourse?**

3. **List three reasons a person should see a doctor regarding sexual health:**

    ❑ _____

    ❑ _____

    ❑ _____

Breaking Up

Alas, not all relationships last, and going through a breakup, whether it's your idea or your partner's, is never, ever fun. There are exactly three ways this can go, dumping, being dumped, or deciding together that it's over and time to move on.

If you have been dumped, there's pretty much only one way to feel: awful. Know right now that you will get over it, but it will take time. In the meantime, having a broken heart is awful, and no one can fix it or make it better. Only time will heal. Until that happens, don't isolate and stay home moping. That doesn't mean you should jump right back out there and starting dating again, but it does mean that you should hang out with friends, call your mom, go to the movies. In time, it will get better.

If you are the one doing the dumping, here's some advice. Never break up on the phone, by text, or by email. That's the chicken way out. Meet with the person, and explain your feelings. Be as nice as you can, while still being honest and direct about the fact that you don't wish to continue a relationship. And don't be cruel and go into all the reasons why — he's loud and sloppy, she's catty and slurps her coffee. Be kind, but firm.

Also, don't try to 'change the rules' of the relationship from a committed, monogamous one to one where you are free to start dating other people, unless you are certain that this is also what the other person wants. If your partner is uncomfortable with being in an open relationship, do not force it. Break it off instead, or you will simply make the other person miserable and jealous. And, no: if the other person is heartbroken, don't ask if you can 'still be friends'. You can't, not right now.

Do remember that for every time you do a 'bad dump" on a partner, the karmic laws will kick in the shins, you'll fall madly in love with someone, and be heartbroken yourself. What goes around comes around, and as hard as it is to do the right thing when you're breaking someone's heart, do it with as much kindness as you possibly can.

Sex and the Internet

Online dating is a good place to find romantic partners. It is also the perfect place to find lonely people to take advantage of. And you are potentially that lonely person. You may think that you are savvy enough and mature enough to know when you are being scammed, but and you may be certain that the person you are communicating with is a real person, who really cares about you. You may think that you are smart enough to avoid these people, but you are not. Trust me: *they do this for a living and they are very good at it.*

There are very dangerous, very intelligent, and very convincing people on the internet who are looking for targets all the time. They 'hook' you with emotional pleas, lots of praise, money, freedom from your current living situation, or offers of sex. Here's how that breaks down:

Crime...	How it happens...
Sexual exploitation	Kidnapping, trafficking, prostitution, posting online photos or videos, 'revenge' porn
Sexual assault	Rape, date rape, coercive sex
Fraud	Money, identity theft, coercion to commit illegal acts
Assault and battery	Hate crimes, assault and theft
Emotional manipulation	'Outing', hate crimes, psychological manipulation and abuse

Rules of the Road

Follow these rules to help ensure your safety online.

NEVER give someone (within three months of communicating with someone):

- ❏ Your full name with middle name
- ❏ Your address
- ❏ Your social security or bank info
- ❏ The name of your school
- ❏ Pictures of yourself

ALWAYS inform your online friends:

❑ That your parents, friends or roommates have access to your computer and know what you are doing online.

If you are hiding someone from your friends and family, or if someone is asking you to hide information from your friends and family, SOMETHING IS WRONG.

Meeting IRL

Ironically, one of the best ways to protect yourself from 'bad players' is to meet them in real life. This immediately cuts out the people who are trying to scam you or trying to fool you into believing they are someone they are not. However, you must be very cautious about how and when to meet people. It's always ideal to go with a friend to meet someone new, but that is not always possible.

ALWAYS arrange:

❑ To meet during the day
❑ To meet in a public place that is busy like a coffee shop (not a park!)
❑ To have the person you are meeting send you a picture of their photo ID before you agree to meet
❑ To have your phone FULLY CHARGED and ON

Send the picture of the photo ID, along with the time and place you are meeting this person, to a family member or trusted friend and tell the person you plan on meeting that you have done so. If they ask the same of you, send it, but block off the license number and street address!

And NEVER:

❑ Get in a car with someone you just met
❑ Go someplace away from other people with someone you just met

Common Scams

Many 'romantic partners' are out for your money or identity, and get to you under the guise of being romantically or sexually interested in you. Here are the most common forms of scams online.

- ❑ **Catfishing** —this is probably the most common dating scam. People pose as interested and interesting dating partners and communicate online with you. They will 'work' you for a long time, maybe even sending you fake photos, and promises of a relationship together. They often ask for money to help them come to visit you, or ask for help with a situation they are in, paying off bills for a sick gramma, or help buying a replacement phone so they can talk to you more. They may also be 'playing' with you just for the 'fun' of it with no intention of ever meeting you.

- ❑ **Phishing** —Typically, phishers find you. You may get an email from them, or a post on Facebook or other social media. Typically, they will tell you that they found your profile online and they want to meet you because you are the perfect mate for them. They may tell you that they are being hurt, that they have access to lots of money, or that they are living in a war-torn country and are trying to get out. Same thing as with catfishing, they have no intention of meeting you. They want your money.

- ❑ **Nigerian Scams** —Both catfishing and phishing are types of Nigerian scams, where a person is identified as a target (you) and some ploy used to get to your money or your credit cards. But, they come in other forms as well. In our business, we have had 'families' from out of the country (typically Asia) who want to bring their child to us for services for two weeks. They will pay any amount, we just need to tell them how much, and they will send us a check. How this plays out is this: they send us a real check, with instructions that it is over the amount because their lawyer also needs a payment, say of $5000. We deposit the check, say for $25,000, write the check for $5000 or wire it, and... the initial check for $25,000 bounces and we are out $5,000 for the check we wrote. There are many, many variations on this, but they all end up the same

- ❑ **Identity Theft** —This is similar, but is on a broader scale. Not only do the scammers have your money, they have access to your accounts (credit cards, bank accounts, PayPal, Amazon, etc) and rack up all sorts of charges in your name. Undoing this type of problem can take years, and seriously damage your credit. Never, ever give anyone access to your accounts! If you want to buy something for someone, buy it yourself. Period.

Online Pornography

Pornography is a hot button for many people, and we are not going to go into any of the moral issues of whether it's good or bad. Instead, let's talk about some pragmatic issues.

- ❑ **Some pornography involves people who are coerced into filmmaking.** Some adult film actors make a conscious choice to work in this industry, and that is their right. However, some people, particularly women, are still compelled to work and have no other options. You have to decide if that is okay with you.

- ❑ **Some pornography involves children.** The law is very clear that no one under the age of 18 should be participating in pornography, as it constitutes child abuse. You might quibble of someone who is 16 or 17, but it is not psychologically healthy, particularly for younger children, to be sexualized at a young age. By watching child pornography, you are in effect encouraging the sexual abuse of children. This is inhumane, and watching this type of porn is illegal.

- ❑ **Some pornography involves people who are not aware they are being filmed.** Some pornography comprises people who are not aware of being filmed. They may be urinating, having sex in their bedrooms, or walking down the street and having a camera pointed up their skirts. Again, you have to decide if you think it's right to invade people's privacy this way. Ask yourself how you would feel if the world could watch you as you defecated in what you thought was the privacy of a bathroom stall at Target. We would argue that it is wrong, and watching this type of pornography encourages this behavior.

- ❑ **Some involves hurting people or, yes, even killing them (snuff films).** I really hope we don't have to describe this one. Enough to say that this is truly sick behavior, and watching this type of thing can damage you. Stay away from it.

Even if you are watching 'good' pornography (no children, consenting adults, no physical violence), watching it too much has negative consequences:

- ❑ In the real world, most men and women do NOT have sex like porn stars, and watching porn can lead to very unrealistic ideas about what real sex is.

- ❑ Porn addiction, where you are no longer capable of having regular sexual relations with real people, is a real thing.

- ❑ Some pornography is very misogynist and can lead men to believe that women are only here for their sexual pleasure as things and can be used however men want. This is not healthy.

In short, if you're going to watch porn, please do so responsibly, and only occasionally. Remember that everyone on those screens is real, and remember that your brain is the biggest sexual organ you have. If you train your brain to only respond to this sort of sexual experience, you jeopardize being able to fully experience the joys of the 'real deal'.

Entertaining

Now that you're a master at social skills and dating, it's time to learn how to have a party! Entertaining simply means having people over (or going out) and having fun. Entertaining can be elaborate or simple. You can entertain every weekend, or once a year. But do try to entertain once in a while. Most people love to go to parties, and love to have fun. Being good at entertaining helps to ensure that you will have a good social life.

Planning a Social Event

Once you have made a few friends, you need to cultivate those friendships over time. One great way to do that is to host events at your home, or at a local venue, even if that venue is a movie theater! Do remember that people are busy, and not everyone you invite will be able to come. Don't take that as a sign you're doing something wrong, necessarily, and keep trying.

1. **Pick a place**. Where are you going to have an event? Will it be a big event, or a little get together? If the gathering will be held in your home,]pick an area for the guests to sit, chat, and eat. Clean the area beforehand and tidy up to ensure that the guests are comfortable and won't be touching any of your personal items (private photos, cell phones, or anything that you aren't comfortable having other people see, touch, or play with).

2. **Decide on a theme or activity**. Will it be for an occasion like a birthday, holiday or sporting event? What about a movie night? Or a Cards Against Humanity night? Or just a pizza and movie night? Deciding on a theme or activity will make planning out the rest of the details much easier.

3. **Determine a date and time for your event**. If it's a birthday party, most people try to have the party on that date, or a date close to the person's actual birthday. Try to pick a date and time where most of your guests are free, keeping in mind work and school schedules. You may not be able to find a time that works for everyone, and that's okay. Promise the people who can't come that you'll do this again soon, and then follow through!

4. **Decide on a budget.** How much money can you comfortably spend? Some events, like going to the movies or having friends over for pizza and games, don't cost much. If you have no budget at all, you can ask people to pay their own way, pitch in, or bring food for everyone to share. There's nothing wrong with that!

5. **Take into consideration who it is you want to invite to your party.** Not everyone wants to dance, not everyone wants to listen to music, not everyone wants to play board games, some people want to talk and relax. You might alter the invitation list to reflect the type of party you are having, and you may want to accommodate for different interests and levels of social comfort with space planning if it is possible.

6. **Start picking the people.** Typically, it's a good idea to only invite people you genuinely like, and not people you think you 'have' to invite. Invite people you would like to get to know better, who will enjoy the activity you've selected, and if you want your party to be big, tell them to bring a friend or two. Get as accurate a count as you can before the party so as to make certain you have the space, parking, food and drink to accommodate everyone.

7. **Make invitations or buy them, or invite people online.** If you're having a party, it's a good idea to hand out actual invitations with the details on them so people have a reminder. Pass them out within a reasonable time frame – not so far in advance that they will forget, and not too close to the date that they may already have plans. Two or three weeks in advance is typically about right. If you plan on instructing your invitees to bring friends, don't send out the invitations too soon or you could end up with a bigger party population than you can handle. If you're going to invite people online, you can consider using Facebook, Eventbrite or another site. If you're having a small get together, you can just send a text reminding people a day or two before.

8. **Determine what food to provide.** If you are going to provide food, make sure to pick foods that your guests like, and make sure you purchase enough. Don't forget beverages, plates,cups, napkins, and utensils!

9. **Music, yes or no?** If you're going to have music, make sure to pick tunes that you think will fit the spirit of your party and your guests. You can also stream music through your favorite player such as Pandora, Spotify, or Amazon.

10. **Clean your house and clean yourself.** Pick the place up, put stuff away, and do at least a light dusting. And don't forget to take a shower, and wear clean clothes! And, make sure there is enough toilet paper! It may sound weird, but you don't want the only memory of your party to be the crisis of running out of toilet paper.

11. **Have some party games set up.** If your invitees don't know each other well yet, grab a copy of Would You Rather, Apples to Apples, Cards Against Humanity, or another quick, fun game to get people warmed up.

12. **Have plans to address rules and guest safety.** No one expects to have things go wrong at a party, but once in a blue moon they just do. Someone gets into a loud argument, someone decides it might be fun to do backflips off the couch, or someone decides to throw a punch. As the host, it is your job to maintain order, and a safe environment for all guests. Quietly but firmly, tell the guests to stop their behaviors immediately or you will call the police. And, follow through if they do not stop. While it's no fun to call the police on your own party, it's better than someone getting hurt or property getting destroyed!

13. **Make sure you have a good time and enjoy it!**

EXERCISE 11 — PLAN AND HOLD YOUR EVENT

Either as a group, or individually, create and hold an event following the above steps. Use the worksheet below to create it.

Event Type/Name:	
Date and Time:	
Location:	
What	**Who's Responsible**
Food:	
Beverages:	
Paper Supplies:	
Music:	
Games/Activities:	
Invitations:	
Invitation List:	

Traditions

When we think about traditions, we tend to think of things like going to church on Christmas Eve, having Thanksgiving dinner at Gramma's, or making matzo with your mom. But traditions can be just about anything – funny or serious. Traditions also give life, and the passage of time, more meaning. And, if the same people are involved in the traditions, it builds a lasting memory between friends and families, and that's really what traditions are about.

When I work with teenagers, I often tell them to start cooking with their parents, and learn their favorite recipes from them. Whether it's meatloaf or moussaka doesn't matter. You can carry forward your family's traditions by learning how to cook favorite dishes for your own friends and family.

It's true that when you leave your parent's home, you are cut off to some extent from the traditions you shared with them. You may still be invited to all of the same events, but you also have the opportunity to start your own traditions. They can be big or small. If you are a Disney fanatic, maybe you'll start making an annual 'pilgrimmage' to Disneyland every spring. Or go to Comic-Con every year. Or grab a bunch of friends and go camping every even numbered summer. It doesn't matter what you do. Only that you do it, and best if you do it regularly to make it a true tradition.

Here's an example. When I was 19 years old, I had a Christmas Party at my home while I was in college. It was such a hit, that I had another party the following year. And then the next, and the next. This upcoming December will mark the 39th annual Holiday Party at my house. Many of the same people (college friends) come year after year. They wouldn't miss it, because it is the only time they get to see each other. It is an event not to be missed.

You can do these things as well. All it takes is a little planning and a little creativity. And who knows, in 40 years, maybe you'll still be having the same party with the same people, too!

EXERCISE 12 — TRADITIONS

What traditions would you like to create, or continue from your family? List three ideas below:

1. _____

2. _____

3. _____

Made in the USA
Middletown, DE
20 June 2023

32474983R00097